Essence of the Psalms

Essence of the Psalms
*Poems Inspired
by the Sacred Text*

Norman M. Chansky

Resource *Publications*
An imprint of *Wipf and Stock Publishers*
199 West 8th Avenue • Eugene OR 97401

ESSENCE OF THE PSALMS
Poems Inspired by the Sacred Text

Copyright © 2008 Norman M. Chansky. All rights reserved. Except for brief quotations in critical publications or reviews, no part of this book may be reproduced in any manner without prior written permission from the publisher. Write: Permissions, Wipf and Stock, 199 W. 8th Ave., Eugene, OR 97401.

ISBN 13: 978-1-55635-500-4

Manufactured in the U.S.A.

*I wish to recognize my sisters Lois and Sonya
who received the same legacy as did I from our parents and teachers and
tailored them to their own lives as did our ancestors.*

*I am especially grateful to my wife Elissa
who is a constant source of inspiration
and to my children Linda, James, Keren, Tamar, and Matthew
who have adapted my legacy and, thereby,
perpetuated the traditions I inherited.
No parent can ask more.*

*I am indebted to Matthew Chansky
of Momentum 18 Graphic Design
for his computer assistance.*

*I am especially grateful to Carrie Wolcott
and Tina Campbell Owens of Wipf and Stock Publishers
for their editorial encouragement and assistance*

*This work honors the nameless poets
who composed the original verses of The Psalms,
the unknown editors who emended them,
and the countless little-known teachers
who for centuries preserved them
and passed them on to future generations as a heritage.
Among these teachers were those
who opened student minds to new meanings
by reconstructing the canonized text
and thereby revealing its essence
in a very personal way to an ever-changing world.*

Contents

Introduction / xi

Section One: Ancient Psalms in Modern Style

Part One / 1

Part Two / 23

Part Three / 41

Part Four / 53

Part Five / 65

Section Two: Modern Psalms / 93

Appendix
Words and Music to Modern Psalms / 113

Introduction

Essence of the Psalms
Spirit of the Sacred Psalms

WHO HAS not been in pain or has not been scared? Who has not suffered loss or has grieved or felt wronged or lost hope or sought healing or has been beset by a foe or has sunk deeply into woe? Pain, fear, grief, anger, despair, hurt, and craving relief are part of the human condition as are remorse, forgiveness, revenge, and atonement. These states are what The Book of Psalms address. They articulate our feelings when we fumble for words. They move us from despair to hope; from hurt to healing; from sight to vision; from setback to triumph, from flaw to virtue, from doubt to faith; from the ordinary to awe; from I to God. The Book of Psalms is a collage of poems of praise, celebrating God, Healer and Bulwark against injustice. They lament suffering, shun evil, decry deceit, bemoan defeat, provide comfort, and offer thanks.

Often accompanied by musical instruments, The Psalms were chanted in the First Temple at least 2600 years ago. Many have been found in the Dead Sea Scrolls, c 150 B.C. Today its poetry using rhyme, assonance, and alliteration bandages our wounds, turning sadness to joy and despair to hope.

Who wrote The Psalms is not known. Reading them is like visiting a museum housing ancient anxieties and sacred virtues. As with any work of art their meanings are personal. One is struck by the fact that similar themes, even identical phrases, are repeated in the 150 poems in the sacred text. The numbering of The Psalms, moreover, is arbitrary.

Pick any psalm, ponder over it, link the text to your life, pause between phrases, and let the words unveil the sacred message, penned by the divinely inspired poet(s). Be moved by it at each pause and release the constraints of reality and soar to a higher spiritual plane. The sacred words will bud within you and you will open a blossom of the sublime beautifying every experience you have. Not only that but you will sow the seeds of wisdom and comfort for yourself today and for generations to come.

There are many translations of The Book of Psalms. Some from Hebrew to Greek and to Latin and then to English and to Arabic and many other tongues. Some English versions are based upon other English translations. Each version has a subtlety that makes it unique. While all versions are similar, nuances of the canonized text impact us in different ways depending on the phrasing of the version, our personal past, current events, and our milieu. The messages we understand today may differ from what the psalmist(s) intended. Yet they are inspiring because they praise God and improve moral life on this planet. We find personal meaning in the sometimes-mystical text.

Whether one takes the The Psalms literally or views the language as metaphors, they are peerless. Blending the bitter and the sweet in their journeys through life, they clearly excite emotions in all peoples: Jewish, Christian, Muslim and nonsectarian. Although at one level the messages of the Ancient Psalms are rooted in the history of Israel, at another level they are universal. They speak to all hurting and joyously grateful peoples across eons of time in every corner of the world at dawn and at dusk in temples, in churches, in mosques, in hospitals, in funeral parlors, in schools, in kitchens, in beds, in wedding halls, on ships and in planes, in a word everywhere.

Today, The Book of Psalms is seen by some as poetry of a bygone era. In its day it was an oasis where people could slake their thirst for moral perfection. It was an antidote to loss of faith; an elixir for imbibing the divine. One aim of my book is to capture the spirit of ancient text. The first section of my book is an adaptation of the texts of 150 biblical poems. Meditations on the original psalms, my work extracts the *essence* of the Psalms using the same poetic styles of the original: rhyme, assonance, alliteration, meter, acrostic, and parallelism. God in my work is gender free, neither a he nor a she but The First Cause, the Font of Mercy, the Source of Wisdom, The One and Only Without Equal.

A poem is abstract, culling images and placing them side by side to create a new idea and a new reality. Be it a psalm of praise, of lament, or of virtue, each poem in this collection beams beauty into the soul to enrich our lives. My work has been to remove the silt of time that has polished the ancient motifs and show that we still talk to a personal God through poetry. It shows that suffering, the child of Hurt, is inevitable. One need not despair because hope is an antidote to woe. Hope is what we cling to. Though scarred, no mortal is rudderless as long as one has faith that with

Introduction

God as The Lodestar one will improve the human condition. That takes courage. Reading these poems will not only nourish that courage but will raise the soul to a loftier level than awe to the Sublime.

Essence of The Psalms is divided into two sections: meditations on the ancient psalms in the Holy Writ and modern verses of praise and petition for the disquiet of our times. The styles of the modern psalms are based on those found in the ancient text. The Appendix contains music for the last new psalm, "Thank You God."

Each poem begins with the *mission* of the Psalmist referred to *as the poet*, and ends with this writer's *message* gleaned from the poem. Mission is in bold face and message is in italics in the text. Furthermore, in this book references to God's Traits and Acts begin with a capital letter to distinguish them from those of mortals.

Norman Chansky, Ph.D.

Section One

Ancient Psalms in Modern Style

Part One

Psalm 1. The Counsel of God Inspires the poet's tongue.

Blessèd are they with joy who walking through life
    Scorn the cheat,
        Shun the sinner,
            And ignore the mocker.
Day and night they are Blessèd
    Who with ardor, faith, and resolve study God's Scriptures
        Which are like the roots of fruit trees nourished and
           sustained
In deep-reaching, fertile ancient streams, and throughout Time renew
        themselves and blossom.

God Guides the pure in heart but Turns
Away from evildoers.

Psalm 2. Wrenching with anguish, the poet poses questions to God.

"Why is there so much anger among the nations?
    Why have so many plotted vain schemes?
Too many rulers counsel hatred
    And lead their people into an abyss of slaughter."
God Replies, "All of My Children are Created Holy and Free.
    The seeds of Mercy and Justice I Sowed in them at the Moment
        of Creation.
You rulers of nations listen to My Words:
    Be wise in your counsel, just in your verdicts, and caring for all
        people everywhere.
Work with others to preserve and improve My World: its peoples, its
        animals, its health, its air."

Worship at the Sacred Mount, Refuge to the
pure in heart and be
redeemed.

Psalm 3. The poet makes known David's feelings while in flight.

How sad am I; how fearful.
    Many foes say that God Has Turned away from me. But that is not true!
    You, God, are my Shield; You, God, Raise my head in dignity.
    When I cry in agony, You Answer me, "I will Protect you from the unruly and vexing hordes."
You Have. You Do. You Will. And my sleep is restful and I awake refreshed.

God You Wrap me in Your Saving Grace and Free me from fear.

Psalm 4. The poet asks God for Mercy to achieve inner peace.

O God of Mercy! Enemies slight me; foes, shame me. Alone was I in my anguish. Cast off!
    I begged; I pleaded. Heed my prayer!
You Listened to my heart and Cleansed my soul.
    Through Your Merciful Love, You Beamed Your Divine Light upon me
And Mended my broken spirit and Wrapped me in Sublime Joy.
    Into the presence of the upright You Brought me.
Now, at night, when I lie down, cloaked in peace, my slumber is calm and safe.

You Dwell within me and I feel safe.

Psalm 5. The poet, tormented wails "Protect me, God".

O God! Hear my voice; Weigh my words.
    I have worries that gnaw at the marrow of my soul
Over which I brood when I go to sleep and upon which I anguish when I awake.
    I am besieged by evildoers whose deeds are ruthless;
I am surrounded by fools whose minds are empty.
    Some rip Your World apart through malice;
Others spoil Your World through neglect. They flood Your World with shame!

Part One

    Praising Your Glorious Name, I humbly seek Your Mercy in
                                                   Your Holy Shrine.
Awed am I by Your Sublime Creation,
    I pray that through Your Kindness I am Shielded from boasters
                                               and cunning frauds.
I pray that You, O Refuge, Teach me fitting and decent ways and
                                       Envelop me with the upright.

              You, God, are my Refuge; You are my Haven.

Psalm 6. The poet, distressed and forlorn, laments, Restore me.

O God! My enemies afflict me; my foes vex me.
    Weak, I sob; anguished, I groan; distraught, I wail.
In my bed tears swell in my eyes; torment thunders in my ears.
    Rebuke me not, I implore; Chastise me not, I plead.
Can the dead honor Your Name? Can a corpse sing Your praises?
    Comfort and Heal me. In Your Mercy Accept my prayers!
Renounce my foes clad in shame; Shelter not they who thrive on guile.
    As long as I live I will honor You and sing praises to Your Name

              Ever will I thank You for Your Bountiful
                      Gifts and Your Merciful Love.

Psalm 7. The poet petitions God for Refuge.

O God! I praise Your Name.
    I have foes who plot to sunder my soul as a lion claws at prey.
Protect me from their wiles; Deliver me from their snares; Spare me
                                       from their ploys.
I have no wish to hurt others but if I deserve Rebuke let it be
                                      Quick and Merciful.
But You, O God, My Judge and Shield, Know of my honesty,
    Grade me on the Divine Scale of Virtue

               Evildoers are snared by their own traps;
                    Shield those who obey You.

Psalm 8. The poet marvels at God's Creation

O God! Daily, I, a speck in Space and a tick in Time,
    Behold Your Splendid Creation:
The Tallest Mountains, the Deepest Oceans,
    And the Lustrous Lights of the Vaulting Heavens.
I ask who am I, a mere mortal, that You Cherish me?
    Who am I, a plain human, that You Esteem me?
Still my foes, I pray to You who Charts the courses of the
    heavenly bodies.
    Crown my soul with Your Majesty and Whisper,
        "You are Sacred verging on the Divine."

O God! Matchless and Magnificent are the
Works of Your Creation.

Psalm 9. The poet praises the Just and Merciful God for the Wonders of Creation.

O God! How Splendid are the Wonder and Mystery of Your Works.
    From the core of our souls we sing Your praises to all nations:
We tell them that You Abound in Mercy;
    That you Listen to the suffering of the oppressed;
That You are a Refuge to the needy;
    And that You Favor those who obey Your Sacred Code of Conduct.
Fairly do You Judge our deeds.
    Warmly do You Welcome all who come to You.
You Enfold all in Purity.
    May the day come soon when evil no longer dwells on the Earth
And those who plot outrage are trapped in their own snares.
    On that day Holiness will Reign.

O God! Ever will we praise Your Splendid
and Sublime Works.

Psalm 10. The poet whose trust in God was flagging asks for God's Mercy.

O God ! In this world filled with pain and torment where are You to
    be found?
Where do You Hide in the midst of so much woe?
The wicked torment the poor;
    The greedy hoard riches yet profane Your Name.

Part One

The haughty boast they will never falter or fail.
    They lie, they curse, they speak guile.
They prey upon the needy like lions who ambush their victims.
      O God! Weigh the plight of the oppressed: the poor, the widows,
                              and the orphan.
Reveal Yourself and Show them Your Mercy.
    Raise up the humble; Aid the helpless; Heal the ailing.

> *O God! Protect the wronged from those*
> *who terrorize. Amen*

Psalm 11. The poet is confident that God is the Refuge for the righteous.

Wherever the righteous walk the wretched wicked lurk in the shadows
    And hurl stones at them.
        There is no place on earth free of vicious villains
Not in dark caves nor on icy mountain tops nor in forest thickets
                  nor in sprawling towns.

> *O God! Haven and Refuge. The pure in heart*
> *are drawn to You.*

Psalm 12. The poet begs God for Help.

O God! Rescue us.
    The faithful are few. Where are they to be found?
        The loyal and honest are too rare. Where do they nest?
All around are uncouth wheedlers, panderers, boasters, and tyrants.
    Their tongues talk treachery; their lips speak lies.
        We run from them to You, God, our Haven.
            Your Words Make us safe. Your Laws Protect us
                from the wicked.

> *O God! Save us! Receive us into Your Refuge.*

Psalm 13. The poet implores God to Grant courage to carry on.

O God! Do You Forget me? Do You Hide from me?
    My troubles are heavy; my sorrows are too many to bear.
My foes rile me; they delight in my ordeals.
      I pray that You Send me an Ounce of Your Strength and a Grain
                          of Your Wisdom.

Constant has been my love for You.
    In Your Mercy You have Saved me in the past. I trust You Will again.
I sing Your praises and honor Your Caring Spirit.
    I lift my voice to God chanting again and again, Save me! Save me!

Psalm 14. The poet, grieving, asks God to Reform the wicked.

The corrupt deny You O God
    The vicious seek to destroy Your Creation.
They rob, murder, and set fire to themselves and to others.
    From Your Divine Realm Frustrate their plans; Thwart their designs.
Shine Your Light and Guide the evildoers toward the paths of Goodness and Purity.
    O God! You are The Refuge of the weak, the ill, the well-to-do, the strong, the robust.
Cradle us in Your Bosom. Kindle the Lamp of Kindness and Fill our souls with Grace
    And all peoples will raise their voices in songs of thanksgiving.
    O God! Your faithful cling to You. Embrace them in love.

Psalm 15. The poet insists that only the righteous earn the security of God's Love.

O God! I ask who may pray in Your Holy Place?
    Who is righteous enough to worship in Your Sacred Space?
Not the one who makes loans and charges high fees
    And not the one who bribes and swears falsely against those without taint.
Only the blameless, those without blemish, who speak no evil, who aid their neighbors.
    Only those who honor You, O God, may worship in Your Sacred Space.
    O God! The pure in soul find Safety and Love in Your Bosom.

Part One

Psalm 16. The poet expresses confidence in God.

O God! You are my Ally; my Partner; my Friend; my Protector;
> my Refuge.

The ways of the unGodly disgust me; I despise the roads
> the wicked walk!

But rooted in The Sacred and anchored in The Pure
> Your Ways Lead me to Perfect Joy; Your Paths Guide me to
>> Good Conscience.

You are as near to me as my right hand; You are the Delight
> of my heart.

> *O Ever Present One Forsake me not,*
>> *Desert me not but Show me*
>> *Your Love.*

Psalm 17. The poet declares innocence and seeks God's Protection.

O God! Nightly You Probe my soul and daily You Take Note of
> my actions.
>> Do I not act justly? Do I not perform good deeds?
>> Am I not without guilt? Am I not free of deceit?
>>> I walk in Your Ways and find You Here, There, and Everywhere.

Listen to my heart that tells You that like wild beasts my foes stalk me
> And seek to rend me to pieces.

But I pray to You, O God of Mercy, Protect all who walk in Your Ways.

> *O God! 'Neath the Shelter of Your Wings*
>> *Protect the upright from their*
>> *foes.*

Psalm 18. The poet thanks God for freedom from foes.

In my distress I, your humble servant, called to You!
> In my anguish I, your lowly subject, prayed to You!

O God! My Rock! My Fortress! My Refuge! My Savior!
> I am righteous; I obey Your Laws.

Hear my cry. Undo the snares that trap me and the cords of Death
> that menace me.
>> Lift me above the storm that rages about me; Rescue me from
>>> foes who lash out at me.

Make fleet my legs; Give courage to my heart;
> Fill my brain with Wisdom; Make meek my soul.

As a bird catches the currents of the wind
   Let me fly from the snare my enemy sets.
As a lion leaps to capture its prey
   Let me scale every hurdle and bravely avert danger.
You Answered and mountains were shaking;
You Replied and the Earth was quaking;
   Then there was a thick darkness in the clouds in the sky
           and a blackness in the waters.
You Freed me from the cords of Death; You Saved me from the abyss
           of the grave.
   *O God! My Shield! I thank You for Protecting
       me. Abide within me forever.*

Based on II Samuel, 22

Psalm 19. The poet prays for God's Guidance.

In the still of the night and in the brilliance of the day
   The Heavenly Hosts Reveal the Glory of God.
How Magnificent is Creation; how Breathtaking is the Cosmos.
   How Glorious are birds, fish, plants, and animals.
All are Perfect and without equal arising from God's Endless Wisdom.
   Noble, Sublime, and Just are God's Laws. They Echo through
           the Cosmic Silence.
They are more precious than gold and sweeter than honey.
   I pray, O God, My Rock, Spare me from my own folly;
Deliver me from my willful habits.
   My Redeemer, Cleanse me of my faults; Purge me of my defects.
       O God! Accept my sincere prayers.

Psalm 20 The poet prays for victory over a foe.

We pray to You with conviction;
   O God, Protect us in our affliction;
       Give us Your Benediction.
Bring success to our noble aim;
   With joy will we victory proclaim;
       And Your Mighty Power in triumph acclaim.
You O God are Just;
   In Your Power, not armed chariots, do we trust;
       Grant us a victory robust.
           We call to You and You Redeem us.

Part One

Psalm 21. The poet thanks God for the gifts to defeat the enemy.

O God! Our foes plot against us
    They fill our lives with woe.
In the bleakest of black yesterdays
    They seek to set this sacred land ablaze.
But Your Love, O God, for Your people is Constant
    And we trust in You.
You Give us Courage and Wisdom to prevail;
    You Help us their monstrous quests to curtail.
You Chase the foes and their seed from our soil; Holy is Your Name.
    Ever do we sing praises for Your Gifts.
O God! O God! We rejoice in Your Strength.
    With victory You Honor our king whose faith in You is abiding

Exalted are You in Your Holy Place.

Psalm 22. The poet prays for God's Comfort.

O God! I am surrounded by foes who disdain You.
    They gloat upon my hardships; they scoff at my sad state.
Like wild beasts they stalk me and plot to maul me.
    No longer do I feel human; I feel despised like a lowly worm
        that is stepped on.
O Protector and Refuge of my forebears!
    Forsake me not. Come to my aid! Rescue me! Redeem me!
I waste away and dissolve in my own tears.
    Spurn not the pleas of the poor and oppressed; Desert not those
        who trust in You.
There will come a day soon when all nations will turn to You.
    My people gather to thank You each night;
And to bless Your Name each day.

O God! All mortals know of Your Justice and
    Mercy and teach their seed.

Psalm 23. The poet's soul belongs to God even in the darkest of days.

O God! Ever my Comfort and my Guide!
>Lacking nothing, I, a humble soul of clay,

Unafraid, lie with Your Blesséd Sons and Daughters By green pastures
>>beside calm waters.

With Mercy You Show me the Right Path to walk;
>With Kindness You Return me to Your Flock.

I am not concerned about what is sure to come;
>What mortal can ever Death's darkness plumb?

But restored am I by Your Love Divine
>And ever will I dwell in Your Sacred Shrine.

>>*O God! You Restore my soul and*
>>>*Give Solace to all.*

Psalm 24. The poet praises the One True God

The world so vast Was by God Created;
And to its dwellers for a twinkling Donated.
>Who does God to the Sacred Mount invite?
>The pure, the honest and the contrite.

They are the ones that the Merciful One Blesses;
They are the ones who with God coalesces
>Because their lives are truly unflawed
>And their souls awed by the One True God.

Open your minds and admit God Divine.
And Cosmic Hosts will enter from the Holy Shrine.

>>*Unlock the gates that dam your souls.*
>>>*Praise God Whom all extols.*

Psalm 25. The poet recites an alphabet of pleas and thanks.

Almighty God, daily does my soul seek You.
>Become my Hope and my Trust.
>>Cancel the schemes of the faithless.
>>>Direct me away from their corrupt paths.

Eager am I for Your Truth.
>Forgive the errors of my Youth;
>>Give Your Love to babes and Your Mercy to the agéd.
>>>Humble I become because You Guide me.

Part One

    I entreat You in my prayers to Set me Free.
        Judge my good deeds and Forgive my wrongs.
            Lonely and broken am I in dark days,
                Make me whole again.
No one consoles me like You Do.
        Open my eyes to see Your Truth.
            Pardon the wrongs I have done to hurt others.
                Redeem my people.
                      Sincerely I thank You for the Goodness
                          You Bestow.

    O God! Teach me the Ways of Holiness.

Psalm 26. The poet, pure in spirit, prays for God's Mercy.

O God! I lead a life of honor; I trust You with all my heart.
    Test me! Probe me! Judge me! You Watch my coming in
                          and my going out.
You know that my mind plots no scheme and never do I
                          Your Name blaspheme.
    My hands take no bribe but help the needy; my mouth speaks no
                          ill except of the greedy.
Sincere is my praise of Your Creation; genuine is my daily meditation.
    Yet I have foes who speak shocking lies and my good
                          name vilifies.
Give me Your Support. Free me in Your Court.

            *Through Your Love am I esteemed; through
                    Your Mercy am I redeemed.*

Psalm 27. The poet is confident that God will protect against any peril.

O God! My Lamp in darkness! My Guide when I slip!
    No person do I fear; no foe do I dread.
My Shield! You Protect me; My Teacher! You Respect me.
    I esteem myself and hold my head high
Even when screaming vultures about me fly.
    You Give me Courage; You Endow me with Strength
And the Spirit to beautify Creation.
    I walk in the Straight Path You Show me.
It leads to Your Shrine
    Where I seek to dwell and bask in Your Wisdom.

>   Hide not from me O God of Mine.
>   Take my hand and Fill my soul with Salvation.
>
>   *Trust in the God becomes valor in the heart.*

Psalm 28. The poet's love of God is enduring.

>   O God! My Rock; my Protector.
>   Are You Blind to those who torment me?
>   Are You Deaf to those who resent me?
>   I trust In You without any qualms.
>   At this moment Quell my anguish;
>   I sorely need Your Aid.
>   At this moment of my oppression
>   I urgently need Your Rescue
>   Listen to my vexation!
>   Reach down from Your Holy Place and Embrace me.
>   My voice sings Your praises;
>   My tongue blesses Your Goodness.
>
>   *God is the Stronghold of all peoples.*

Psalm 29. The poet listens for the Voice of God

>   The Voice of God is heard in the Joyous chattering of the bird,
>   In the sizzling Burst of a lightning flash, in the earsplitting
>   Blast of a thunder crash,
>   In the raucous Roar of the roiling seas, in the silent Zephyr that
>   sways the trees,
>   In the mournful Lowing of the calf, in the muffled Murmur
>   of the tall giraffe.
>   God's Voice is Strong; God's Voice is Calm.
>   God's Voice is Healing; God's Voice is Balm.
>   From God does Strength Flow: to the mighty and to the low.
>
>   *God's Voice Entwines all dwellers on earth*
>   *with Peace Sublime.*

Part One

Psalm 30. The poet thanks God for Rescue

O God! I was ill, pained and anguished.
    How I ached. How I suffered.
I thought Death was near;
    I heard my enemies cheer. Were You in hiding? Can I praise
        Your Name in Death?
    I appealed to You and You Listened.
You Healed me and Returned me to the living.
    My suffering was for a moment; my torment was fleeting.
I endured; I persevered. I devoted my being to serve You.
    Now I sing Your praises; now I dance to the tunes
        the Angels play.
Who but the living can extol Your Name? Who but the mortal
        can give You honor?
    My fears dissolved and songs of thanks flowed from my soul.

        O God! How Gracious are You! You Surround
        us with Solace.

Psalm 31. The poet prays for the persecuted.

O God! My Rescue and My Refuge!
    Listen to the inner chamber of my soul.
I am weary with worrisome woes yet filled with Hope
    Because You, my Fortress, will Protect me.
And You, my Healer, will Mend me.
    You Free me from the snares my enemies have set.
I have entrusted my soul to You
    I have committed my being to Your Keeping.
No matter what others say
    You my God, Font of Mercy, Source of Salvation,
        Wellspring of Goodness,
Foundation of all that is Good and Just, Root of Kindness,
    Beam Your Radiance on Your humble servant.
Blesséd Are You Who Comforts us with Kindness.

        Divine Comfort awaits the faithful.

Psalm 32. The poet seeks healing for a wounded soul.

When I was by life frustrated
    And I Your Good Way violated,
My soul became taxed with guilt
    And my spirit sagged and began to wilt.
How sorry was I for what I had done;
    How I doomed myself to oblivion.
I moaned, I groaned, I shed many a tear;
    My confessions were candid; my admissions, sincere.
'Though mortal I am and error prone
    Weak am I without backbone
I prayed that You Teach me Your Good Way
    So that I will never again go astray.
You Heard my self-damnations;
    You Listened to my meditations.
Then You Absolved me with Mercy Divine;
    Then You Cherished me with Charity Sublime.
When in Your Ways I became immersed
    My sorrows to dust were then dispersed.
Then hope arose within my heart
    And my soul did then a better world chart.

I no longer fear the night and once again
I know delight.

Psalm 33. The poet proclaims that the upright merit joy in God.

Rejoice O Virtuous Ones! O Upright Ones be praised!
    God Spoke and the Heavens were formed; God Breathed
        and Cosmic Lights appeared.
Seas gathered and dispersed; lakes closed and filled with fish.
    Water cleansed, fed, and nourished life;
All life is from God's Decree,
    "Let there be."
We adore the Creator; we revere the Wonders of the Founder.
    Many are the ways to show our thanks:
With stringéd instruments, with singing, with dancing,
        even with silence.
    The songs must be earnest; the music must rise from the soul.

Part One

The dancing is simple; the silence is sacred.
> But the the most sublime way to honor God is through acts of kindness.

Let all peoples revere The Almighty; let all dwellers on earth honor The Merciful God.
And they will be Blessed and they will be Happy.

> *These we emulate in God we emulate:*
> *Righteousness, Justice, and Mercy.*

Psalm 34. The poet recites a list of guides to approach God's Goodness.

Adore The Almighty! Our God exists!
> Bless The Eternal One every day and in every way.

Combine justice with mercy.
> Declare God's Goodness when the sun rises and when it sets.

Exalt God's Name at home; exalt God's Name in the streets.
> Fear no foes for God Grants you strength.

Gather the Courage that God Gave your heart.
> Honor God through your charity.

Impure is the tongue that speaks deceit; always tell the truth.
> Justice is everyone's birthright.

Kindness heals the distressed.
> Laud God during leisure and exalt God while at work.

Many are the ills of the upright but God is their Comfort.
> Nourish your love of God with acts of mercy.

Open your minds to the Miracles of Creation.
> Pardon your defects and those of your fathers and mothers.

Quell the urge to condemn sisters and brothers.
> Remember the good in yourself and in others.

Shun what is hateful and pursue what is good.
> Thank God, Refuge and Redeemer, for the Gifts of Creation.

Use your powers to improve the world.
> Voice kind thoughts.

Who does not love life and cherish a future filled with goodness?
> Yearn for God's Redemption.

Zenith is God's Divinity.

> *Our God Exists and is our Light.*

Psalm 35. The poet pleads with God to come to the aid of the persecuted.

O God! What have I done that so many torment me?
    Why do they want to uproot me?
Why am I charged with horrible crimes?
    Bribed witnesses accuse me of evil.
Without cause they chide me; for no reason they deride me.
    They devise pretexts to abase me; they plot ruses to debase me.
You, My God, Who Watch over the oppressed and the poor;
    You, My God, Who Shelter the sick and the distressed,
Listen to my fervent pleas; Hear me proclaiming praises to You.
Do You not Notice my persecution?
    Does not my agony Move You?
Hide not from me! Save me!
    Cast them away like chaff that seek to enslave me.
Frustrate their aim of harassing me;
    Clothe in infamy those shaming me.
And with all my being I say
    Who is like You who Cares for the poor, the needy,
                  and the distressed?

You are My Witness. Remain Silent
no longer.

Psalm 36. The poet extols the Grace of God to all who know suffering.

O God! Author of Life! Creator of Light!
    There are those in whom evil abides who bring misery
                  to so many.
There are those in whom vice is the highest good.
    How they pollute Your Creation; how slyly they scheme
                  each aberration.
Theirs is a world of disdain and of destruction; Yours is a World of
                  Grace, Mercy and Renewal.
    As the Cosmos expands so does Your Charity;
As the Universe unfolds so does Your Charity Spread to all in need
                  of Your Love.
    Paragon of Goodness and Model of Justice, You Fervently
                  Shelter the oppressed.
You Give them water to quench their thirst;
    You Give them food to satisfy their hunger;

Part One

   You Give them Pleasure to brighten their spirits.
      You Give them Friendship.
>*O God! You Gird the humble with Light and*
>*they reflect Your Goodness.*

Psalm 37. The poet ponders over the problem of evil and lists maxims and cures.

Anguish not when witnessing wrongs.
   Be patient with the slow pace of justice.
      Cease from anger lest you do yourself bodily harm.
        Delight in God who Listens to all prayers.
     Envy not the evildoers though they prosper.
  Free yourself from self-righteousness; others will see your deceit.
God Notices wrongdoers and Weeps.
    Humble yourself before God and plant peace of mind.
       In time, the wicked wither like chaff in the wind.
        Join hands with others in pursuit of justice
          and mercy.
     Keep faith despite failure.
Look to God for Comfort and Refuge.
Many achieve glory though they deserve it not.
    Notice the upright and be like them.
       Omnipotent is God alone; humans lack that Strength.
        Pardon the flaws of others and they will
          pardon yours.
      Quarrel with few; find grounds to agree upon.
  Rage begets rage.
Spare others from despair as God Spares you from sorrow.
    Trust in God even when you are forlorn.
       Understand that there is both good and evil
         in this world.
        Venom flows from the mouths of the evildoers;
          honey, from the righteous.
      Wallow not in self-pity; work, instead, to improve
         the plight of the needy.
Xenophobia corrodes God's World.
    Yearn for peace, lasting peace.
>*The zealot is not pious but perverts*
>*God's Laws.*

Psalm 38. The poet examines previous wrongs and repents.

O God! Listen to my plea.
> My flesh burns and withers.

It feels as if Your Arrows are Piercing me.
> I have reviewed my past

And find much that I regret.
> My back is bent carrying my burden.

I mourn for the days that I have lost forever.
> My heart trembles and I have no strength left.

Once I had friends but they have run away from me;
> Some even plot to do me more harm than I have already done to myself.

I pray do not Forsake me. Draw near to me. Hurry to my side.

> *I pledge my life to follow Your Ways because You are my Salvation.*

Psalm 39. The poet speaks of the quality of life and of mortality.

O God! Life's strains fill me with consternation;
> Anger grows out of my frustration.

Yet I silence my tongue;
> I am still young.

But I ponder when will my end come;
> I am speechless; I am dumb.

Am I but a puff in a fleeting cloud?
> Am I but a faint voice in a noisy crowd?

Who am I? What is to become of me?
> God! Heed my cry!

Listen to my sigh.
> I anguish, I suffer, I am filled with woe.

When I am dead where will I go?
> Is it to Give Sorrow that You Create?

Is there no way You Will my suffering Abate?
> I pray that You do not Ignore me.

I plead that You do not Abhor me.
> I am confused and vexed

I am bewildered and perplexed.
> Why Give me life if You will Take it away?

Is Death the fate of Your Child of clay?

> *O God! When I become dust who will know that You are Kind and Just?*

Part One

Psalm 40. The poet prays to God for Deliverance.
    O God! My soul is pocked with anguish; my heart is heavy
                                          with blame.
    My purse is empty; my clothes are threadbare.
Too many are the hardships that befall me. Too many are those
                                        who scoff at me.
    Others deny You; others ridicule You.
But I trust in You; I believe in the Endless Wonders You Create.
    I practice mercy to ease the burdens of others;
I pursue compassion to give comfort to others.
    I pray that you Give me strength to cope with my woe;
I pray that you Show me how to carry on and grow. My hope is in You,
                        O God; Save me.

        O God! I pray for my Redemption.
              Do not delay.

Psalm 41. The poet, afflicted, cries out in agony.
O God! I am ill. I suffer in body and in mind.
    You Watch over the oppressed
And to all afflicted Are Kind
    I plead, I beg "Console the distressed".

Pain stabs me like a knife
    Yet even my dearest friends whisper slurs.
They cannot wait until I am Taken from life.
    Every human errs.

And with deepest remorse I repent
    My imperfection.
Often I have done wrongs without intent
    I pray for Your Protection.

Heal me. Undo the schemes of my foes.
    Be Gracious unto me
Free me from my woes
    Grant me time before Your Final Decree.

        Restore me Dear God Blesséd among the
            nations in every age.

Part Two

Part Two

Psalm 42. The poet laments the fate of being Exiled from God.

All about me I hear scoffers sneer at me, "Where is your God?"
    I am sad. My spirits are down. I moan and I groan.
I know that You, O God, are my Salvation; I know that You,
                                  O God, are my Refuge.
    I ask where Are You when I am so oppressed?
I ask why have I been Dispossessed?
    What questions! You Are Everywhere and Always.
        And I am here a mere vowel in Your Book.
You Crown mountains with glimmering snow; You Cap the sea
                                  with billowing waves.
    Who but You through Mercy Saves all who seek You,
        All who Your Kindness pursue.
You Tint the sky copper at dusk and Adorn the sun gold at dawn.
    I am in a drought like the parched fawn
Yearning to slake my thirst.
    I entreat You to Give hope to my arid soul.
Then as before a hymn will rise from my throat
    And praises to You will I devote.

                O God! Sit by me in Your Temple as I pray
                          for renewal of Your Creation.

Psalm 43. The poet, though feeling abandoned, does not give up hope.

O God! I am so confused. I am attacked from all sides;
    Jeered at, mocked, ridiculed.
O Advocate and Refuge, where are You to be found?
    Have I fallen from Your Grace? Do You not See my sad face?
Be my Judge and Vindicate me. I have kept Your commandments!
    Despite my desperation, despite my vexation,
I sincerely sing praises to Your Name; I proclaim Your Greatness
    Because like sweet music of the lyre You Inspire good works.

                O God! Be not silent. Answer me with
                        Divine Music.

Psalm 44. The poet retells of God's great deeds and pleads for Intervention.

O God! Of Your Greatness have our forebears told
    And have Your Splendor extolled.
Your Mighty Hand once Drove out the foe
    Your Caring Heart Softened our woe.
But now where have You Gone?
    Why has Your Presence been Withdrawn?
You once Put our enemies to shame
    And we blessed Your Glorious Name.
But now we are haunted;
    Now we are taunted
By enemies who have taken away our land.
    We have from our own country been banned.
They mock us in their songs
    Why are You not Righting these wrongs?
O God, our Foundation!
    Despite our humiliation
Your Goodness we proclaim
    And bless Your Holy Name.

We pray that You Your people Embrace
*   and their enemies Efface.*

Psalm 45. The poet glorifies the king on his wedding day.

What an honor it is to speak praises of one as royal as you.
    O that my tongue would utter clever phrases to describe
        with art your proper due.
Among men you are the most radiant and fair; among heroes
        no one is bolder;
    Your bravery is historic and rare; no one carries a burden with
        a stronger shoulder.
Your kingdom is a gift quite rare; you are the ideal of what is just;
    Your cunning wisdom uplifts, earning Your people's trust.
Your queen equals you in splendor; her beauty, too, is unmatched
    Superlative of her gender! How happy are you to be to
        her attached.
And bridesmaids with song and dance in gowns sequined in gold
    Perfume the air expanse with scents exquisite to behold

Part Two

From which passion sprouts. Majesties! Love each other
           and bring forth an heir.
 Be kind and fair to each other and your goodness
           with others share.

     The fame of a royal husband and wife,
         imparted by my modest
         rhyme,

    Is founded upon cherishing life and will
        inspire all throughout time.

Psalm 46. The poet proclaims that God Is a Citadel of nations

Trouble abounds but God Is our Refuge
 Tragedies afflict but God Is our Asylum.
Who but God Can Make the earth shake?
 Who but God Can Topple mountains
And then Drop them into the sea and Make it rage?
 Mighty God Thunders and the earth melts.
Then comes This Message from on High
 To a world that has gone awry:
Stop war! Set your weapons on fire.
 And when peace rises out of the ashes,
Gaze upon the river of suffering that has turned to joy
 And admire the path to the holy temple
On which all may walk hand in hand
 And spread harmony throughout the land.

     God is Strength and Haven to all
        peacemakers.

Psalm 47. The poet proclaims God's Majesty.

Sound the ram's horn; clap your hands; shout praises;
        sing beautiful songs.
 For God is Supreme King of kings who Cherishes
        all children of Abraham
And has Given them a holy land as their eternal heritage
 To be stewards of Nature and protectors of all peoples.

     God, Majestic Master of the Cosmos,
       Bestowed Zion to Abraham's
       seed.

Psalm 48. The poet celebrates God's Sparing of Jerusalem from the foe.

We the Children of Zion were safe in the Bosom of God,
                                  the All-Powerful ,
    Unseen but Loving, Just, and Abounding in Mercy.
Then Assyrian kings swarming like raging mosquitos
    Ready to suck the marrow from our souls
Scoffed at God and prepared to assault us.
        A Mighty Storm Arose Making trees to Sway and mountains
                                to Tremble and Collapse.
The stunned kings quivered in fright and fled; panic spread among
                                the raiders.
    Zion's sons and daughters cheered and sang praises to God
                                for Saving them.
The Temple still stands! The Temple still stands!
    People everywhere throughout time will look to Zion Gilded
                                by God's Kindness.

                God's Loving-kindness inspires righteousness.

Psalm 49. The poet proclaims the wisdom of the ages.

People everywhere listen to my voice;
    All you who follow me hear my words
Whether you are rich or poor, high born or low,
    You cannot haggle with God about mortality.
Both coward and brave are fated to find eternal rest
    In a quiet, dark grave but God Redeems the souls
                                of the virtuous.

                Life like wealth waxes and wanes but
                    the Blessings of God are
                constant.

Psalm 50. The poet urges the willful to repent and become upright.

In the human heart is much deceit
    For which sacrifices do not atone.
When you swindle and when you cheat
    It is you that I, Your God, Disown.
The animals of the forest are Mine
    And ample are the fruits of the field.
Upon Zion does My Day Star Shine;
    The righteous are My Shield.

Part Two

I Call to you both east and west
    Vex Me no more;
Worship Me with reverence and zest
    Let the goodness within you soar.
Ignore Me not is My advice
    Lest you will be Destroyed
Thanks I Seek, not sacrifice.
    Then My Pardon will be deployed.

God's Touch Is in all Creation, Goodness
Is the World's Foundation.
Offer love with devotion profound,
and God's Blessings
Will Abound.

Psalm 51. The poet appeals to God to Cleanse the wayward.

O God! I was thoughtless and have done wrong; my will
    was weak, not strong.
    Cleanse me of transgression; Purge me of indiscretion.
My deeds have been black as night but I am sincerely contrite.
    I pray that You Purify my heart and good works to my
    soul Impart.
Your Pardon I beg Deploy; I pray that You Fill my life with joy.
    Your Holy Spirit has Taught me what I should; I vow to teach
    others The Divine Good.

O God! I praise Your Holy Name and Your
Glory proclaim.

Psalm 52. The poet scolds the slanderer

Do you think that you who are moneyed
    Have license with a razor sharp tongue
To lie, defame, abuse and boast?
    God will Oust you from your house
    Then will Pluck you from your tent
Unless you follow the Sacred Laws and repent.
    The righteous will say in Merciful God give your trust.
    Our Refuge, Haven, and Inspiration
    Is Loving and Is Just.

The saintly are sturdy like an olive tree
planted in God's House.

Psalm 53. The poet appalled by Israel's plight begs all to abide by God's Laws.

God Watched from the Divine Abode
    And Beheld much moral decay.
Few adhered to the Sacred Code
    Of Decency and Caring. Dismay
Pervaded God's Mood.
    And the Almighty Scattered
The troops of those who would feud
    With the Children of Israel, battered
By the ruthless schemes of those
    Fools who doubt God's Existence.
For them there will be no repose;
    Only fear and turbulence.

O that tormented Israel will one day find deliverance!

O that an era of peace will unveil the good in people and undo ignorance!

Psalm 54. The poet seeks God's Help to Thwart evildoers.

O God! I am sounding an alarm!
    There are strangers about
Who seek to do me harm.
    These are times of moral drought.
O God! Hear my plea.
    Undo their evil intent.
O God! Listen to my agony
    And their vile schemes Prevent.

*God's Help Sustains me; God's Mercy Makes me strong
I embrace Divine Charity and give thanks in song.*

Part Two

Psalm 55. The poet again asks God to Punish Evildoers.

My enemies oppress me; my foes belittle me.
    What mischief they spread; how they fill my heart with dread.
O God! Do you Hear? Are You Listening with Your Ear?
    Watch their every act of cruelty. Watch me writhe in agony.
I feel such dismay; Give me wings to fly away.
    Direct me; Protect me.
Day and night I pray that my anguish Will You Allay.
    Humble every foe; Give peace a chance to grow.
In You who are Just do I trust.

> *God Unchain us from our misery;*
> *God Sustain us with*
> *Your Charity.*

Psalm 56. The poet, saved from distress by God, gives thanks.

O God! How sorely my foes afflict me! How unfairly my
                              enemies depict me!
    How unjustly they convict me! How much harm they do me!
Daily they set traps; daily their voices roar like thunderclaps;
    Daily they slap my face to debase me before the crowd.
Once I was afraid. Once I cringed when they degraded me.
    But I trusted in You and my fear dissolved.
Tears cascading from my eyes spatter Your Record Book.
    Like diamonds they sparkle.
When will my suffering abate?
    My memory not only tingles with sorrow but daily reminds
                              me that You are my Savior.
Humbly I pray that You Make me brave;
    Meekly I appeal to You that You Help me punish those who
                              would enslave me.
May they whose deeds You Record as putrid and disgusting
                              quickly turn to dust.
    No matter how dire my plight in You God will I ever trust.

> *I will remember the path to Glory and to Joy*
> *is through God's Virtue.*

Psalm 57. The poet is certain that God is a Refuge and Protector.

O God! How fierce are my foes; they lie in wait for me.
    Like beasts they wait to pounce on me.
Like hunters they wait to spear me.
    Like trappers they wait to ensnare me.
But You Shelter me beneath the Shadow of Your Wings
    And Thwart their designs.
I sing praises to You,
    Steadfast and Merciful God
Whose Glory Covers the Earth.

Although mortals maltreat others God
Protects us from great harm.

Psalm 58. The poet condemns unjust rulers.

There are people who are evil all of their lives;
    Even when they are young their tongues speak lies,
Poison drips from their lips.
    They stuff their ears so that they do not hear truth.
And when they go before the kings of the jungle of wild mortals
    Their errant ways are judged acceptable, even perfect.
The deeds of the judge and the judged are equally corrupt.
    May they vanish like sewer bilge; may they be uprooted
        like weeds.
God only Rewards the righteous.
    In this world God is the Only Just Ruler.

The fate of the corrupt is a prison of their
own making;
The reward of the upright is God's Grace.

Psalm 59. The poet besieged by raging ravagers prays for God's Intervention.

O God! I strive to be upright to treat every one fairly.
    Yet there are some who howl like wild dogs and thirst for my
        blood day and night.
O God of Mercy, Refuge and Protection, Dull their swords,
    Quench the fire of their words and Show us all the path
        to Perfection.
Slay not the foe but Drain away their rage

Part Two

> Show them the Beauty of Your Creation and Cleanse
> > the world of woe.
> > > *Sing hymns of praise to the Compassionate*
> > > *God, Source of our strength.*

Psalm 60. The poet pleads with God to Help the humbled people of Israel.

O God! Our foes are strong and have devastated us.
> They have broken our spirit; they have stifled the song
> > We sing to You with reverence and ardor.

We have been split, smashed, defeated.
> Our souls are gashed. Heal us!
> > Are You Angry? Have You Deserted us?

Are we to be Wiped out among the nations?
> Take us back! Take us back!
> > With You as our Guide will we triumph;

Victory is ours with You at our side.
> On that day will our valor be restored
> > And will we share Your Wisdom with the world.

> > > *The beleaguered tribes of Israel are split*
> > > > *asunder by enemy weapons;*
> > > *Their spirits sag but will be restored through*
> > > > *God's Wisdom and Support.*

Psalm 61. The poet yearns to return to Zion where God's Spirit Dwells.

O God! I weep; Hear my sobs.
> O God! I cry; Taste my tears.

My spirit soars in Zion;
> My soul finds peace in Jerusalem.

But I am elsewhere not there.
> My despair is a nightmare.

O God! Be my Refuge;
> Set me 'neath Your Wings.

How ardently I pray to You
> How fervently I pledge my loyalty to You.

I am grateful to You for the gift of life;
> Daily do I recite thanks to You for the Heritage Given at Sinai.

> > *Our lives are crowned with the Glory of God.*

Psalm 62. The poet proclaims that only God is a Refuge for humanity.

I am harassed; I am terrorized.
>Patiently do I wait for You God, my Refuge;
>>Without complaint, will I cling to the hope that my
>>>Salvation is approaching.

I know that You God will Rescue me
>From those who bless me with their lips
>>But curse me with their hearts.

Those of low degree are vain;
>Those of high degree are deceitful.
>>Together they weigh no more than a puff of breath.

Some rob. But how enduring is their wealth?
>Others use force to gain their ends.
>>But how they defile Creation.

My faith is in You, Merciful God Who is Strong and Who Soothes
>>my troubled soul.

God Renders Mercy according to one's deeds.

Psalm 63. The poet exiled from Zion longs to return to the Sanctuary.

Banished by those I love, I have vanished from my home
>Wandering the wilderness without direction seeking Your
>>Loving Protection.

My soul thirsts for Your Kindness; my entire being yearns for
>Your Mercy.

>I fill the marrow of my being with Your Blessings.

At night I pray that You Enfold me in Your Wings and Bring
>me home.

>I praise Your Name.

Send those who speak lies about me to the remote regions of
>Your Realm
>>Let them do no one harm anymore.

God Raises our spirits and Brings us home.

Part Two

Psalm 64. The poet prays for Divine Justice

O God! I find myself among hateful people
    Whose words are like barbed arrows dipped in poison.
They frighten me; they terrify me.
    They lay snares to entrap the innocent;
They place lures to ambush the virtuous.
    O God! I cry to You
Save me from their wiles;
    Protect me from their schemes.
The righteous seek Your Refuge;
    The upright praise Your Name.

        O God! Font of Justice Foil the plotters of evil.

Psalm 65. The poet describes how manifest are God's Great Ways.

O God Eternal! People far and near
    Praise Your Mighty Deeds:
Who but You Can Raise mountains to lofty heights?
    Who but You Can Calm the raging seas?
Who but You Can Quell rebellious people?
    Who but You Can Bring rain
And Crown the meadows with crops
    Which sustain all of Your Creatures:
Insects, animals, and people?
    We, the weak and flawed,
Overwhelmed by our failings too many to mention,
    Seek to dwell in Your Holy Place.
Humbly we pray that You Forgive us.
    And with Abundant Love
Grant us victory in our struggles.
    With songs of joy we praise Your Name.

        Almighty God Who Are The Source of
                Strength and Cause of
                Creation,
      Tame the tempest and Absolve
                the blemished.

Psalm 66. The poet says all to praise God, Giver of Life, who Listens to our pleas.

O peoples of the earth! Sing a joyful song unto God.

Praise God's Name Divine! Enter the Sacred Shrine
And exult in God's Awesome Deeds. You foes of goodness cower and cringe

Because of God's Mighty Power. On any day at any hour
God Can Turn the sea to dry land and Can Carve a path in the sand.

You who wrong sister and brother learn from God to get along with each other.

Avoid rancor, vengeance, and strife then praise God who Gave you Life

Let the Holy Spirit your hearts Purify and your souls Glorify.
Think only warm and tender thoughts in your mind.
And thank God by doing deeds kind.

Then your prayers will be sincere And God will Listen and Deem you dear.

God, All-Powerful, is Caring and Shows all the Right Path to follow.

Psalm 67. The poet declares the Gracious God's Greatness for which praise is due.

O God! With fairness do You Rule the world and Reveal to all
the Right Path.
You are Kind to us and Save us from wrongdoing and
Help us curb our wrath.
You have Blessed us with abundant harvest. For this we humble
peoples praise Your Name,
Revered in every place and at every time.
O that the words of my mouth and the Psalms in my heart
May always please You, my Hope, my Comfort,
and my Deliverer.

With joy do peoples praise the Loving God.

Part Two

Psalm 68. The poet cries out to God, Savior of the oppressed.

O God! There are too many who prey upon the innocent;
    There are too many who abuse the fragile.
O God! You are a Witness to such injustice;
    You Eye with Compassion the oppressed.
You Protect with Mercy the orphan, the widow, the lonely,
                                    the depressed
    And those unfairly in prison confined.
O God! Bring justice to those who wrong the innocent.
    Dissolve them like wax of a candle aflame;
Scatter them to the winds like ashes from a fire.
    God! Know how we are denounced without cause;
O God! Know how we are debased by the nations.
    Shield us from scoundrels;
        Defend us against rogues.
           Gladden the hearts of the righteous!
Abide in the souls of the virtuous!
    You Bring rains to the parched earth
        And bounty to the harvest.
            Your Light Guides the wanderers
                    in the wilderness;
                Your Power gives courage to the
                          defenders of the desert people.
        We sing praises to You for saving us;
            We chant hymns to You for Giving us Courage.
    Your Deeds are like silver;
Your Feats are like gold.
    Who but You God will Abide forever?
        Who but You God is Hope Eternal?
            O God! Show Your Abundant Kindness to us;
                Spare us who are in distress.
                    Cherish us; Deliver us.
    We will praise Your Name from mountain top to seashore.
We will praise Your Name in every generation.

*   God Eternal, Witness to human cruelty,*
*   Deliver the oppressed from the depths*
*   of despair.*

Psalm 69. The pained poet pleads with God to mend the people's condition.

O God! My eyes are empty of tears;
    My throat is parched from pleading.
I call upon You to Save me through Your Goodness and Mercy.
    Because I sink deeper and deeper in mire;
A flood washes over me.
    My enemies are many, more than the hairs on my head;
They eddy higher than clouds in the sky.
    Everywhere do I seek You;
        Do You Hide from me?
            In You my faith is deep;
                In You my trust is profound.
                      Because of my love for You my
                        own brothers mock me;
                Because of my devotion to You sots
                    taunt me!
        I am in despair; life is a nightmare.
      My pain pleads with You to Drown my foes in
            Your Wrath;
    My yellow badge of shame pleads with You to Strike down those
            who torment me.
Save me to rebuild Your Holy City and to renew Your Heritage.
            In every place and in every era we
                extol Your Name.

*   Insulted by the nations the voice of Zion asks*
*   God for relief and support.*

Psalm 70. The poet asks that God promptly Save Zion.

O God! There are those among the nations
    Who seek to cast me into a prison pit
And there to torture me until my raw wounds fester.
    Hurry God! Delay not. Save me, Your poor and needy servant.
Frustrate and Disgrace the plotters.
    I join those who rejoice in You
And bless Your Name.

*   Tormented by the nations the voice of Zion*
*   asks for God's Speed.*

Part Two

Psalm 71. The poet asks God to Listen to the stirrings of the heart.

O God! Human scum vex me; they crush my spirit.
    I suffer in agony;
My soul is in distress.
    O my Refuge Rescue me.
O my Savior Deliver me.
    You are my Hope; You are my Light.
My foes say that you have Forsaken me.
    Many declare that I am not in Your favor.
They scoff that You turn a Deaf Ear to my pleas.
    Hasten to my side. I am growing old and my strength wanes.
Do not Abandon me. Listen to my pleas. Desert me not.
    Punish those who seek to injure me.
In my distress Revive me; in my suffering Heal me.
    Daily do I bless Your Name;
Each day I walk in the Righteous Path You Designed.
    Every moment I marvel at Your Creation and praise Your Name.

Renounced by foes the poet asks God for help.

Psalm 72. The poet asks God to Guide all rulers on Earth.

O God! Many children are oppressed;
    Many peoples are distressed.
So many are hungry and in need;
    So many are victims of an evil deed.
They can be saved by the rulers of the world
    Around whom Your Wisdom is daily Unfurled.
Imbue these rulers with Acts of clemency
    Implant in their hearts Seeds of Charity.
Water the seeds and virtue will grow;
    Enrich their homes and peace will flow.
Show them how to banish fear;
    Unveil to them how to hold each soul dear.
Reveal to them Your Wondrous Way
    And Your peoples will be Blessed every day.

Rulers who truly care for their people
promote peace in the world.

Part Three

73. The poet, in a weak moment, envies the villain.

O God! How I envied the ill-gotten gains of rogues.
>Their bodies are strong; their burdens, few; their wiles, many
>>and crafty without equal.
>They clothe themselves in violence;

And although their deeds are loathsome, they feel no guilt.
>Instead, medals of pride decorate their chests.

But some day You will Mete out Justice to them.
>And although I envied them and stumbled from the Right Path

When I entered Your Holy Shrine, Refuge for anguished souls,
>I received Your Forgiveness and asked that you Guide me in the
>>ways of the upright.
>You are Good to those whose hearts are pure.

>>*The ways of scoundrels are tempting but do*
>>>*not bring God's blessings.*

Psalm 74. The poet asks if God Rejects Zion for all time.

O God! We are like abandoned doves,
>Once we were Your Chosen ones, Your Beloved among
>>the nations.

Marauders have come and destroyed our nests
>And have smashed Your Holy Shrine.

They have torched the trees
>And stepped on us like fleas.

All we have is tribulation;
>In Whom are we to find Salvation?

Not in our foes who curse Your Name;
>Not in our enemies who Your Name Defame.

Ignore us not; Neglect us not.
>We keep the laws that You Gave to Moses;

We keep the pact that You Made with the prophets.
>Invading hordes plan to ruin us;

Raiding droves seek to destroy us.
>We pray to You who thrust away the waters,

And Blessed our sons and daughters,
> Rescue us and Rekindle the Light unto the nations.
>> *Our enemies are many. Save us Your*
>> *holy people.*

Psalm 75. The poet offers thanks for the Blessings God Bestows.
O God! How Dear You Are: How Near You Are.
> We praise You daily.
You, Glorious God, Perform Great Deeds.
> With sublime love we bless You;
We, mere clay in Your hands, marvel
> At how You Keep the world together
And vow to follow Your Laws.
> We tell the boaster
Do not swell in pride because you are mere rabble
> Who babble about your greatness.
Each of you is a smudge on the soul of humanity
> And God will Judge you Harshly.
Your power will dwindle
> But the power of the righteous will increase.
>> *God, the source of all Good, is praised.*
>> *People of virtue will flourish, not so*
>> *the wicked.*

Psalm 76. The poet proclaims God, The Almighty, Just Judge of all.
Known far and near is the Name of God.
> O God, Occupant of every atom of the cosmos,
Your Strength is without equal.
> The most menacing mortals cower upon hearing Your Name;
>> The most sinister of warriors melt in fear of Your Power.
>>> Break their arrows and Bend their shields and Make a mockery of their bravery.
> They are stunned;
>> They are numbed by Your Might.
>>> Everlasting is Your Majesty;
>> Eternal is Your Glory.
> You are the Savior of the oppressed;

Part Three

You are the Redeemer of the dispossessed.

> *God, Perfect Judge, Protects the innocent and Instills fear in preying foes.*

Psalm 77. The poet recalls the Mighty Deeds God Performed.

I languish at night; I anguish by day.
    Where Are You God? Why Are You Mute? Remember Your Love,
        Your Mercy, Your Compassion.
    Now I feel alone; now I feel deserted.
Abandon me not; Reject not Your distressed child.
    I marvel at Your Creation, Your Holiness, Your Strength.
I shake like the quaking earth, I rumble like clapping thunder, I scud
        like streaking lightning.
    Weary, I pray that You Comfort my soul
And Lead me back to Your Favor as You once Led Moses and Aaron.
    I will reflect on Your Goodness each day and will sing Your
        praises each night.

> *Despite The All Loving being distant,*
> *I seek God's Goodness and Revelation.*

Psalm. 78. The poet praises God's Grace but chides those who flout God's Ways.

Listen to God's Message; heed God's Words.
    These Words were heard by our forbears;
These Words were heard by their forbears and theirs before them.
    These Words are those of the pact with the patriarchs;
These Words were witnessed by the matriarchs.
    Teach Them to your children and they will teach Them to theirs:
God performs Wondrous Deeds;
    Observe God's Laws.
Trust in and be faithful to God
    Who Led your ancestors out of Egypt
And Fed them in the wilderness
    And who Led them to the land of Zion
And Nurtured them in their homeland.
    Be not willful but follow the straight path of virtue.

Remember that some of the stalwart died because they rebelled;
    Not so the children of Judah's tribe.
God Sustained them and through them Built a Sacred Shrine.
    God Tended them Lovingly like shepherds tend their flocks.

God Seeks the righteous and Rewards them.

Psalm 79. The poet prays for God's Deliverance

So many nations have invaded our land
    And defiled our Holy Shrine
And debased the remains of the slaughtered victims
    And tortured the oppressed
Whose blood runs through the streets of Zion
    And whose groans rise to the Heavens.
Nearby neighbors scold us; nearby nations scoff at us.
    They taunt us where is your God?
How long must we be the ridicule of the world?
    When, O God, will Your Anger Cease?
When, O God, will You Rescue and Redeem us?
    When will you Spill Your Wrath on the nations
That accost Your people?
    Show us Forgiveness, Mercy, and Kindness.
We, Your people, will praise Your Name forever.

The tormented of Zion appeal to God
for Compassion
and Deliverance.

Psalm. 80. The poet appeals to God to Revive the battered nation.

O God! Guardian of Israel!
    Listen to our aching hearts.
We sup on our sorrow; we taste our tears.
    Mute Your Anger and Shine Your Light upon us.
Save us. Redeem us.
    Too many nations scoff at us
Because we believed in You and kept Your Ways.
    But it was You who Raised the mountains and opened the seas;
It was You who Cleared the land for planting and Made
                        the rivers flow

Part Three

  And the vineyards grow.
How fragile our souls have become.
Return us to Your Favor; Show us Your Kindness. We are
            Your Community.
  In unity forever will we praise Your Name.

     The distressed people of the world pray
        for God's Protection.

Psalm 81. The poet sings a joyful ode to God.

Blow the trumpet; beat the timbrel;
  Strum the lyre; pluck the harp.
Dance with delight and roar with joy
  Whenever the new moon appears.
Exalt in God! Exalt in God!
  It is an edict from The Divine; it is the Law of the Almighty.
Jacob obeyed It and passed It on to Joseph
  And Joseph passed It to all generations that followed.
God does not Hide; God is Ever Present.
  Worship the Just One and pray to the Compassionate One
Who Brought you out of Egypt into freedom
  And Defeated your enemies on the battlefield
And Fed you with the finest grain
  And Sweetened your lives with the sweetest honey.
Turn not your hearts away from God but incline your ears to
           The Sacred.
  Direct your feet in the Ways of the Righteous.

    Celebrate the Light of The Moon with cheer
      and honor God,
      The Deliverer.

Psalm 82. The poet praises God, The Supreme.

In the heart of the Holiest Shrine God Presides over all beings
         human and Divine.
  You and your seed, make it your creed
To be kind to the poor, the orphan, and those in need.
  They are Warned not to be immersed in deceit
Or enchanted by their own conceit.
  The very core of Creation reels

When a servant of God wheels and deals
>   With bribe takers and trouble makers.
Act justly with all or like mortals you will fall
>   Into the grave. Help God Discover ways to Heal every
>>   aching soul
And make all peoples whole.
>   God, Supreme Ruler of this world! Gather Your children
>>   and their souls Redeem.

> *Those who serve God must strive for
> higher goals.*

Psalm 83. The poet asks God to Spare the people from their foes.

O God! Listen to our foes.
>   They scheme secret plans to destroy us.
They gather north, south, and east of us
>   And whisper, "let's wipe them out".
They seek to erase our names from history.
>   Bring a storm upon them; Set their plans on fire;
Spread their ashes to the four winds.
>   Humble them; Harass them.
Shame them; Disgrace them.
>   Teach them that You Alone are God,
Supreme Ruler of the universe.

> *The foes of God must not prevail but must
> be defeated.*

Psalm 84. The poet yearns to return to God's Sacred Shrine.

O God! How my soul aches to dwell in Your Holy Place
>   Where I can join so many in praise of Your Great Works.
There will I be Blessed;
>   There will I feel as safe as a bird in its nest.
O God! Not only are You my Shield
>   But the Source of Grace and Glory,
A Stronghold against all that bodes ill in this world.
>   The rewards of Creation are for the upright.
How Blessed are they who trust in You day and night.

> *God Keeps the good and pure safe.*

Part Three

Psalm 85. The poet prays for the well-being of Zion.

O God! How Kind You Are;
    How Gentle Are Your Ways.
You Pardoned Your Children's wrongs;
    You Undid Your Wrath
And Made the bleak earth thrive again.
    Once again we are in need;
Once again we are besieged;
    Once again we call upon Your Help.
Make us strong again;
    Revive us. Save us.
Show us Your Love, a Love that does not fail.
    We follow Your Ways to sow peace.
Your Grace will Sprinkle gently from Above;
    A Spark of Zeal of Your Splendor will rise up
From the core of our souls
    And Reflect Your Goodness throughout the human family.
Truth and Justice will embrace each other.
    And we will praise Your Name forever.

> *We ask God who Plants Blessings to Unfold*
> *Peace and Justice.*

Psalm 86. The poet, true to God, prays for help.

O God! I, Your servant, devout but in need,
    Pray that You my doleful prayer heed.
I am beset by many a violent foe
    Who does not Your Good Ways care to know.
Never do they Your Great Works extol
    Or in Your School of Wisdom do enroll.
O God of Mercy, Full of Grace,
    Help me my follies to erase.
No thing can to You compare;
    Sacred is Your Divinity and also Rare.
Comfort me with a Sign that I will become free
    Of the wrath of those filled with calumny.
And every day will I renew
    My deep felt thanks O God to You.

> *God Spare me from those who seek to destroy*
> *the marrow of my soul.*

Psalm 87. The poet praises the holy city of Jerusalem.

Is there another place in all of the world quite as splendid and sublime
                                            as Jerusalem ?
    Strong as a lion; gentle as a lamb.
Founded on the Holy Mount whose Sacred Spirit is the Fount
    Of all that is Glorious for every nation.
The Light of Zion is for all peoples to rejoice in.
    And God will Choose all the righteous from every homeland
                                          to improve Creation.
And people throughout history
    Will sing and dance to honor Zion's Spirit, source of
                                          our Blessings.

*   The Spirit of Zion ennobles all peoples.*

Psalm 88. The poet pleads for Relief.

O God! My Savior! My every cell is sick; my will is waning.
    Long have I suffered; No longer can I abide my pain.
My life is filled with darkness; my every thought is bleak.
    I am shunned by friends; gloomy are the words I speak.
You Crush me with Fury; You Beset me with Troubles.
    Your Wrath Ignites my despair; Your Apathy Withers my soul.
Can I sing Your Praises in my grave? Can I extol You when I am
                                          in the pit?
    I feel discarded like trash; my mouth chokes on the dregs
                                          of my ebbing life.
My eyes are weak from crying; my body languishes in dying.
    I beg You to listen to my prayers; I appeal to You to
                                          Send me Relief.
I have not deserted You; Cast me not away.

*   Despite despair the poet holds out hope that*
*   Rescue Will Come from God.*

Part Three

Psalm 89. The poet bemoans the coming national calamity.

O God filled with Mercy, Flower of Goodness,
    The Heavens declare Your Devotion and Your Glory.
Who but You Calms the swelling seas?
    Who but You Forms the Heavenly Crown and brightens it
                                          with stars?
Who but You Has Formed the fertile earth and Filled it with life?
    How Constant is Your Love; how Endless is Your Kindness.
We sing to You, Rock of Our Safekeeping.
    You Quashed the foe time and time again; You Crushed those
                                        who assailed us.
    You Made a pact with David's seed;
You Made a pledge to David's line
    That You Will Be Just and Upright
And You Have Kept Your Promise.
    In return You Expected the Children of Zion to keep Your Laws.
And 'though you Chastised them when they strayed
    You did not Withdraw Your Love.
But now we are faced with a fearful foe
    Who taunts and mocks us and threatens to destroy us.
Revive Your Steadfast Love
    And from the snow peaked mountain in the north
To the sun baked desert in the south
    We will replace our lament with everlasting praise of Your Name.
                    will be faithful to You for ever
                    and ever. Amen! Amen!

            God will Protect the children of Israel from
                    those who beset them.

Part Four

90. The poet praises God's Mighty Deeds that Bless frail humanity.

Ere the cosmos was formed
    And the mountains grew
And seas swarming with life
    Arose from the deep
And land loomed from the sea
    There was You, O God, Divine Splendor,
Which Gave Life to all creatures.
    Dust at first then bodies, souls, and mind,
Your Children are like blades of grass
    That shoot up in the morning,
Grasping the Goodness of the sun to thrive at noon,
    And then wither and die at night.
They share Your Goodness with nearby lives,
    Sustaining them but also obtaining some of their merit.
You Gave Your Creatures choices which life paths to follow.
    Some pursue routes that raise the level of the human soul;
Others wander along the ways of the wayward.
    At the end of each road is Your Embrace.
God ! We seek not Your Wrath but Your Wisdom.
    Gladden our hearts in the morning light,
Help us grow at noon,
    And Show us Mercy in the dark of night.
May the Blessings of Your Love Favor us with joy
    And Guide our hearts, minds, and hands to perform good deeds.
                      Amen

Brief are the days of the mortal
Fill them with worthy efforts which enrich
*   the Grandeur of Creation.*

Psalm 91. The poet assures the listeners of God's Protection.

O God! My Refuge. You are like a fortress.
    Because of You am I full of hope; because of You am I
                      Wrapped in trust.

You sent Guardians to Watch over me;
    You sent Divine Shields to Protect me.
They fend off the mauling lion;
    They spare me from the venom of snakes.
They keep me from the scourges at night;
    They Keep me safe from snares during the day.
My heart beats with gladness;
    My soul soars aloft with joy.
Listen to the thanks of my mouth;
    Hear the blessings of my heart.
And through the Silence of Your Divine Realm I hear The Words
    "I am Your God and You are My Child."

We dwell in the shadow of the Almighty,
our Shelter.

Psalm 92. The poet thanks God for Creation.

This song we sing on Sabbath day
    As we Kind God to You we pray.
The stringéd lute and harp resound
    To bless You God wheree'er You're Found.

How Great are the Works of Your Creation;
    How Firmly You've Made the World's foundation.
Like palm trees splendid to behold
    You've Made the good with boons untold.

The works that You Deem kind and right
    Will Teach the children of Your Might and Light.
Each day they'll receive Your Perfect Love and True
    But the wicked will receive their deserve'd due.

God is The Paragon of what is right to do.

Psalm 93. The poet celebrates God Sublime.

I sing to You, O God, Nobly Crowned,
    Girded with Strength,
Who in the Beginning Formed the World,
    And Set Its Laws in Motion.

All the Voices of Nature
    Sing Your Praises:

Part Four

The roar of the oceans rolling toward the shore
    And the harmony of the stars resounding in the heavens.

Daily we unveil our souls to witness Your Glory;
    And are Wrapped in Your Abundant Love.
O God Divine we praise Your Name
    And in Your Sacred Shrine become Holy.

The Eternal God Nobly brings Divinity
to those seeking It.

Psalm 94. The poet pleads for Divine Justice.

O God! Good people are hurt;
    The virtuous are trampled upon like dirt.
While the wicked reign
    Widows, orphans and strangers are slain.
The arrogant slap the faces of the upright;
    How they scoff at their plight.
They are wild animals. Brutes
    Laying out their evil pursuits.
Do they not know that You God Taste the tears of the oppressed?
    Do they not know that You God Feel the woe of the distressed?
The evildoers sneer, " Your god ignores you."
    They believe not that The True God will Give them their due.
They weave a wicked web to trap the pure in dread
    But are ensnared themselves instead.
God's Mercy Supports those without flaw;
    God's Love Surrounds those who keep The Law.

Despite the wrongs of the powerful, trust
in God's Justice.

Psalm 95. The poet calls the people to prayer

Good people! Extol God with elation;
    Praise The Eternal Who has no peer; give thanks to God
        Whom all revere:
    Author of Creation; Rock of Salvation;
Composer of Astral Melody. Author of Cosmic Harmony.
    Teacher and Guide Whose Laws Provide rules for all to live by.

Look to God for Justice and Mercy and become virtuous.
> Do not be like the people of the desert
Who forsook The Law and from God's Ways did withdraw.
> Look instead to the Ruler of the world from the deepest depths
>> of seas, waves uncurled,
To the steepest mountains, peaks snow crowned with glistening sun
>> which the eyes astound.
> Extol God with joy unbound.

*God is Paragon of all that is Great
in the universe.*

Psalm 96. The poet praises God Judge of all.

With a loving heart sing unto God a new melody;
> Let a sacred song soar from your soul.
Let it echo with God's Glory;
> Let it reign like God's Majesty.
Let it extol God's Beauty;
> Let it praise God's Strength.
Blesséd is the Wise Creator,
> Paragon of What is Right and Fair.
Tell all to revere God;
> Tell all that the world is firm;
>> Tell all to listen to the songs the stars sing
>>> And the melodies of birds on the wing;
Tell all to listen to the rustle of the trees
> And to hearken to the sound of the gentle breeze.
>> Tell all to ponder the grasses verdant
>>> And to reflect on every flower fragrant.
Then they will know of God's Greatness
> And will bless the Just and Merciful One.

*All peoples of the world revere God,
the Wise, the Just.*

Psalm 97. The poet praises the Majesty of God

Hearken to the Splendid Voice;
> Let all dwellers on Earth in its Sound rejoice.
With Majesty does God Reign
> In Mystic Ways which none can explain.

It Speaks of what is Right and Just
    And Asks of all in God to Trust.

Hearken to the Splendid Voice;
    Let all dwellers on Earth to its Sound rejoice.
Absorb the Light of the One Divine
    And enter into the Holy Shrine.
Fleeting is the mortal's life
    Filled with sadness and heaped with strife.

Hearken to the Splendid Voice;
    Let all dwellers on Earth in its Sound rejoice.
Shun evil ways and become untainted;
    Follow God's Laws and join the Sainted.
For the pious has God's Light been sown;
    To all people of good will God's Voice be known.

God is Distant yet Near and Guides us
to walk the Right Path.

Psalm 98. The poet praises the Divine Author of Justice

Good people! Sing a new song unto God.
    Sing it sweetly; sing it from the heart.
All nations know God is merciful, pure, and just.
    All peoples proclaim in God their trust.
Strum the lyres, blow the horns
    Hear the ocean roar and the river slap against the shore.
Their music praises God all Nature adores.
    Behold God has come to Judge the world with Mercy
        and Justice.

Through music does one reach God.

Psalm 99. The poet praises Holy God.

Tremble O you nations;
    Quiver with awe all dwellers on earth.
The Majestic One is Exalted above all earthly kings;
    The Holy One Reigns Supreme.
Leaders of old called upon God
    Who Answered in a Pillar of Cloud,

"Obey My Laws"
    And the Mighty, Just, and Forgiving One
Escorted them in the Right Path
    And Led the pilgrims in the Sacred Ways.
O you dwellers on earth
    Ascend the Holy Hill and Humbly praise God.

From days of yore Zion's leaders embraced
God in their hearts and souls.

Psalm 100. The poet asks peoples everywhere to praise God.

All dwellers on earth
    Worship together with joy.
Praise the One and Only God.
    Light the Sacred Flame;
Bless God's Holy Name.
    O God, Fount of Mercy,
Your Truth endures forever.

All nations join together to give thanks
to God.

Psalm 101. The poet lists rules of good conduct.

O God! I raise my voice unto You;
    I sing a hymn praising Your Mercy and Your Justice.
Cast out my evil bents: Soften my cranky heart.
    The path to Your Holy City is paved with pure thoughts
        and noble actions.
I walk upon it with my head held high.
    I beseech You Banish the venomous and vile who slander;
I entreat You Expel the pride-preened base who ever tell lies.
    Welcome those with chaste hearts to Your Holy City
And they will help You Mend the fragile world You so Love.

The Just and Merciful God Envelops the
humble in heart.

Part Four

Psalm 102. The poet prays to God for help.

Alone am I; afflicted by lack; despised by neighbors;
                                        denounced by foes.
  My head is on fire with fever; my soul burns with rage.
      My name is a curse and despised everywhere
                                    in the universe.
Some set my body on fire; some erase my place in history.
  I cry in torment; Do You Hear me? I writhe in pain;
                                    Do You See me?
      Tears curdle my milk; mold ferments my bread.
            Ghosts haunt my dreams; phantoms invade
                              my waking hours.
Like a distraught bird lost in the desert I find no oasis
  Yet I thirst for You.
            I pray Do Not Shorten my days before I
                  complete my mission,
            The mission You Gave me.
Show me Your Mercy; Rescue me; Redeem me.
  Return me from exile; Restore me; Comfort me.
      O Time! Close not Your Gates so soon upon my life.
        O Sun! Shine Your Golden Face upon me
            for years to come.
O God, My God! Together we will heal the world.
  I am wretched. Hear my groans. Heed my moans.
      Together we will rebuild the homeland you Promised
            those who came before me.
You are my Polestar;
  You are my Light when the night is dark.
    Look at me God; Hear my voice.
        Let me live in peace; Return me to Zion;
            There Your Spirit dwells in every
                dust-filled rock;
                    There Your Soul Abides in
                        every droplet of water.
Show me Your Mercy; Enfold me in Your Kindness.
  Then all peoples will revere Your Name; then all nations will
            acclaim Your Fame.
      All kingdoms on earth will praise You; all creatures
            on earth will serve You.

Harmony will blossom and virtue will flourish.
In the next generation who will Hand down Your Will to all
yet to be born?
O God ! You will Outlast Your every Creation. You are
Eternal; all else is finite.
You Endure forever.
I worship You; I sing Your praises.

All will adore the Everlasting God and
will live in dignity.

Psalm 103. The poet sing praises to God.

O God! Loving God!
I sow blessings in my innermost core
And praise unfolds from the marrow of my soul.
When I pray, You Hear me;
When I stray, You Forgive me.
Like a father to his children
You Are Kind and Tender.
You Bless us with Love
From Your Abode Above.
You Care for the oppressed; You Comfort the distressed.
You Soothe; You Cure;
You Teach us to be Pure.
From North Pole To South Pole
You Make broken mortals whole
And they revere Your Name
From the nearest to the furthest reaches of Heaven
Celestial hosts Your Greatness Proclaim.

God's Greatness Knows no bounds.

Psalm 104. The poet praises God: Creator and Provider.

O God Who Folded the day into night and Emptied the night
Of Darkness and Brought forth Light
To Guide all Creatures
And toward whose Glow
Plants turn and grow.

O God Who Wed Oxygen to Hydrogen
> To form water Which trickles down mountain ravines
>> To quench the thirst of all living beings
>>> And nourish them so they may flourish.

O God Who Set this planet in motion
> About Its Sun and Moon to mark Time.
>> O God Who set the Earth on solid foundation
>>> And Whose Creation Provides
>>>> Havens for birds, shelters for fish, shrines for the devout,
>>>>> and oases for pilgrims.

O God who Gathers huddling clouds
> And Stretches them into a heavenly canopy
>> Through expanding Space.

We praise You; we bless You.
> Everlasting and Eternal One,
>> More August than any mortal monarch,
>>> Robed in Majesty are You;
>>>> Clothed in Splendor are You.
>>>>> How Great Are Your Works;
>>>>> How Blessed is my soul.

None can compare with the Architect
of the Universe.

Psalm 105. The poet declares that God is faithful to Israel.

Give thanks to God Whose Sacred Works are everywhere seen.
> Praise God with joyous song serene
>> And laud all that is Divine.

Recall God's Promise to the ancients
> To Give the land of Canaan to Judah and his brothers.
>> Recall that Joseph, Isaac's grandson,
>>> Once in slavery enchained,
>>>> Reigned as provisions governor
>>>>> When a famine befell his father's homeland
>>>>> And his kin was to Egypt drawn
>>>>>> To abide in a land of plenty.
>>>>>>> In peace they dwelt for many years.

Then a tyrant king provoked them to tears
    With hard labor and with jeers.
Then a son of Israel arose, Moses by name,
    Who through firm but calm words tried to tame
        The king's heart. But failed.
            He begged the king to let his people go. The king refused.
Then God Ravaged Egypt with frogs, gnats, hail, and wind.
    To no avail.
        Under the cloak of darkness Moses led his people out of Egypt.
        Into a wilderness where food and water was found
    As the Children of Israel were Canaan bound
To keep God's Laws and teach them to peoples every where.
                Praise Be to God!

*   God Chose the seeds of Abraham*
*   and Sarah to build Zion*
*   And there to obey God's Laws.*

Psalm 106. The poet confesses Israel's wrongs and seeks to mend its ways.
What mortal is endowed with fitting words to reveal God's Mighty Acts?
    Who has speech precise enough to portray the Depth and Texture
            of God's Mercy?
    Are there phrases to describe the Marvels and Wonders
        God has Wrought?
How often had our forebears turned their backs on God?
    How often after being Pardoned did they return to perverse ways?
At the Sea of Reeds where the foe was drowned;
    In the Wilderness where they were manna fed;
        At Mount Sinai where God's Words were etched in stone;
            When a calf was cast from golden jewels;
                At altars where their own children were sacrificed
                    to Baal.
        Again and again did You, God, Redeem us
    And Spared a heritage of bondage to our people
                in despair.
Your Legacy of Justice, Kindness, and Hope Endures Forever.

*   Blessed are they who follow in God's Ways.*

Part Five

Psalm 107. The poet thanks God for Redeeming the people of Israel.

A.

No matter which direction we went we battled a ferocious foe.
    Save us! Save us! We humbly prayed; our hearts faltered;
                              we were quite afraid
        That we would be left to die witnessed only by an
                              azure sky.
But God, You Heard our voices sincere,
    The voices of people who are to You so dear.
        Our hungry were Fed;
            Our thirsty, to water Led;
                Our homeless, a haven Granted
                      And our roots there,
                          deeply planted.
We wanderers were Redeemed and by You, God, truly Esteemed.
    We give thanks to You God Whose Kindness
                Endures forever.

B.

How gloomy is exile; no prison is more vile.
    At every corner there is duress. You, God, Heard our distress
And Broke the chains that made bodies bleed and our melancholy
                        souls mercifully Freed
    To walk toward Your Light and follow the Path of the Upright.
        We give thanks to You God Whose Kindness
                  Endures forever.

C.

We strayed from the Righteous Path and were smitten by Your
                            Rending Wrath.
    No food could we digest; serene slumber was a hopeless quest.
        We wailed; we ailed;
            We repented; You Relented.

> Our fate was Unsealed and through You
> were we healed.
>
> *We give thanks to You God Whose Kindness
> Endures forever.*
>
> *God Spares those in need and Restores
> the downcast and afflicted.*

Psalm 108. The poet thanks God for victory.

With steadfast heart I sing
 That my people are free at last;
The once silent psalter and harp
 Awake and praise the dawn.
Great is Your Mercy
 Everlasting, Your Truth.
Your Grandeur Exalts the heavens;
 Your Glory Fills the earth.
You Deliver us from our foes:
 Edom. Philistia, Moab and those yet to be.
You Inspire us to gain courage;
 Through You we triumph and will be free.

> *With God, Our Protector, we resume
> our lives.*

Psalm 109. The poet, anguished, prays that the foes of Israel will be chastened.

O God! Look at what is happening to Your Nation;
 Be not Silent.
I am surrounded by vicious mobs.
 I am kind to them and they scathe me with volleys of curse;
  I bless them and they send salvos of curses at me;
   I speak truth and they deceive me;
    I build them up and they
     tear me down.
      And they have no cause; they have
       no grounds.

Part Five

    It pains me to ask this of You;
        It hurts me to plead with You
            That You Erase their names from history.
                Widow their wives,
                      Orphan their children,
                              And Make them homeless wanderers
                                    begging for food.
O God! Look at us.
    We wither away, we are mere shadows at dusk.
    We are taunted; we are haunted.
            O God, Defender of the needy,
        Save Your Nation.

            Scorned, the poet seeks revenge for hateful
                      neighbors
            And redemption for his nation.

Psalm 110. The poet says that God Will Help the king defeat Israel's foes.

The Word of God Came to my master, the king.
    Honored are you to be My Partner.
We will be joined by the valiant youth of Zion and will humble the foe.
    All will know that together we will prevail and in majesty will
                                    you reign.
Drink from the Sacred Stream and revive your resolve
        And become humane in treating those who provoke
                                  and sting you.

                God Inspires strength in the people.

Psalm 111. The poet praises God's Wondrous Works.

O God! I thank You with all my heart for the Marvelous Gift
                                    of Creation.
I offer thanks in the forum of the upright
        Who delight in and follow Your Glorious, Majestic, and
                                  Superb Laws.
    You Sustain the people of the Covenant
To whom The Land of Zion was Given as a heritage forever. Halleuyah.
                            May You Be Praised.

                Reverence for God's Sacred Name is the
                          source of wisdom.

Psalm 112. The poet praises the upright who embody God's Design for mortals.

Adored Is God!
    Blesséd are they who revere God's Name;
Children of the Blesséd are praised who
    Delight in God's Precepts.
Everlasting is the fame of the upright.
    Faithful are the pious.
Gracious and kind are the devout.
    Honored are they who trust in God.
Immense is God's Mercy,
    Judging all with Kindness.
Light streams through the darkness for the holy.
    Mighty are they who do not lend money for profit.
Never neglect the needy.   Oppose evil.
    Quell vexing foes.   Rescue the fallen.
Serve God gladly.   Trust in God's Love.
    Undo mortal misdeeds.   Value life
                                                above all.

Work together with God to improve this
world is as easy as A,B,C.

Psalm 113. The poet presents a message for the millennium.

From east to west
    All God's Children are Blessed.
Enthroned on High watching the world going awry
    From too much frivolity and not enough equality
God through Sacred Powers Wills order to arise from chaos
    In a New World. These shall be unfurled:
Poor men will sit as equals with princely brothers
    And barren wives shall sit as equals with nursing mothers.
Slaying soldiers shall mourn their slain
    And blasphemers will God no longer profane.
Philosophers will learn wisdom from the hayseed
    And the falsely accused will be redressed and freed.
The hungry will have food to eat
    And the homeless will be sheltered from cold and heat.

The sick will have medical care
> And on the lips of all will be a grateful prayer.

> *Love will replace hate and each child*
> *will grow up to be great.*

Psalm 114. The poet recalls the rapture when the people of Israel left Egypt.
When Israel was from bondage freed
> And they the stranger's tongue no longer spoke
They prayed that God would them Lead
> For a Sense of Awe in them awoke.
How Nature at that moment was whirling
> The waters rolled back and the seas rose high
Hills and mounts like lambs were twirling
> To tell the world God is Adonai. (Adonai-Hebrew Name for God)
Why, waters, do you flee?
> Why, lambs, do you dance?
To tell the world that Israel's free

> *And to enlarge God's Sacred Expanse.*

> *With God and Israel as partners, water can*
> *flow and slake the thirsty.*

Psalm 115. The poet condemns as powerless gods formed by human hands.
O God! Glory is not ours but Yours!
> Nations taunt us and ask where is your God?
Our God, Unseen but Ever-present, is not wrought by human hands.
> Yet Is, Was, and Will be Here, There, and Everywhere.
Ours is not a God of carved mouth that speaks not;
> Or of etched eyes that see not;
Or of grooved ears that hear not;
> Or of sculpted nose that smells not;
Or of molded hand that feels not;
> Or of cast feet that walk not.
Our God is Creator, Shield, and Merciful Judge.
> Our God is Sublime and by all revered;

Those who truly exalt God are Blessed with health, family,
                              and prosperity.
  Only the living can praise God through their prayers.
Not those who lie silently in the grave.

*   God is Timeless and Ever present:*
*   the Font of Blessings.*

Psalm 116. The poet thanks God for good health.

Woe attached to me like a leech,
    Sucking the very marrow of my soul.
All about me was trouble and sorrow.
      Then I prayed to God with heart most devout
          And with the remaining vigor of my waning spirit.
            Help me! Spare me!
                Send me not to the netherworld.
Then a Bright Light, A Mere Speck,
    Scintillated on the horizon.
        It was Wisdom! It was Mercy. It was Justice.
          Wondrous Warmth Embraced me.
            Comfort Fell upon me;
        God's Love Surrounded me; God Heard my
                anguish; God Knew my pain.
    Thank You God! You Delivered me.
Even though I once spoke ill of others,
Saying you lie, my sisters and brothers,
    It was in haste; ineptly timed; poorly placed.
      You God Forgave me.
        In the presence of all
I lift the cup of Salvation and Speak God's Holy Name in Awe.

*   Thanks to God Divine Intervenes*
*   for the desperate.*

Psalm 117. The poet bids all to honor God

All nations on Earth extol God's Truth;
    The entire cosmos praise God's Mercy.
        Halleluyah. Every person praise God's Name.

*   We bless The Merciful God.*

Part Five

Psalm 118. The poet praises God's everlasting Kindness.

   Hateful people surrounded me like angry bees
      And I called to You God in my distress.
         Set me free! Set me free!
            Then a Divine Fire Came and Burned
                    the bees to ashes.
         And I was Freed.
             I sang out, Give thanks to God.
I told the priests, Give thanks to God.
   I told the people of Israel, Give thanks to God.
      I told all who are upright in every land and in
         every time
      Give thanks to God Whose Mercy Endures forever.
Trust not for salvation in any mortal—even a prince
   Instead believe in the Unseen God
      Who, though Chastens, also Rescues and Frees
         the lonely from doom.
      Open, O gates of righteousness
         And I will enter singing thanks to God,
            My Savior.
I am Israel, the stone despised by the masons,
   That keeps God's Sanctuary secure.
      What a marvelous day to celebrate God's Glory.
Rejoice and be glad.
      We beseech You God to Save us now.
       We beseech You God to Make us prosper.
         Blesséd be all who praise the Holy Name of God
           Whose Mercy endures forever.

           God Redeems The scions of Israel
               wherever they are found.

Psalm 119. The poet praises God's Glorious Ways and asks for Salvation.

1. O God! Blesséd are they who walk in Your Sacred Path
   They obey Your Statutes, Your Law.
They are the upright! Admire them; they are without flaw.

2. O God! I carry Your Words in my heart
   Wherever I go
Whether gladdened by joy or saddened by woe.

3. O God! Open my eyes
    That I may see
The Wondrous Things You've Granted me.

4. O God! At times my soul is heavy with qualms
    Because I don't fully grasp Your Ways.
Let me behold the Marvels in Your every Sacred Phrase.

5. O God! Let me climb the Ladder of Your Statutes;
    I will step joyously tread by tread.
Give me understanding and never will I know dread.

6. O God! Instill in me Your Mercy
    For I suffer from those who taunt
Yet ever do I serve You. Your Ways have become my wont.

7. O God! The words of foes batter my soul
    But Your Words Comfort me in my affliction
Though I am an ordinary pilgrim Your Law is my conviction.

8. O God! Indignation burns within me
    Because of they who forsake The Law.
Agitation quivers my fragile soul because too few regard You with awe.

9. O God! I wake at every hour
    To scan my lacks, my dearth.
You are all I ever sought; Your Mercy Fills the earth.

10. O God! Once I erred and became afflicted
    Then I took Your Statutes to heart.
Now neither silver nor gold can tempt me from Your Sublime
                                    Wisdom to depart.

11. O God ! Your Words Give hope
    Because Your Judgments are Just.
Your Mercies are Tender; in Your Perfect Laws do I trust.

12. O God! My soul pines for Salvation;
    Your Wisdom descends from Heaven in the sun's rays.
Although taunted am I by those around me, I will never forsake
                                    Your Ways.

Part Five

13. O God! You Ordained the Laws of Nature;
    Your Precepts Guiding mortals are unsurpassed.
Although every purpose has an ending, like Earth, Your Laws
                                                remain steadfast.

14. O God! Your Wise Words are sweeter than honey;
    Never am I vexed.
You are my only Teacher; the Torah my only text.
                                (Torah-Holy Writ)

15. O God! Although the wicked lay traps for me
    And engage me in strife.
I am not led astray for Your Words Guide me through life.

16. O God! Shield me from hypocrites;
    They are like putrid currents in a gale.
Wrap me in Your Teachings and Purity, not dross, will prevail.

17. O God! I have studied Your Law
    And to falsehood am I blind.
Prevent the haughty from oppressing me; Rid the world of
                                                their kind. Amen.

18. O God! Your Words Gleam with Light;
    On Understanding do they Shine.
Direct my feet to Your Wisdom. I accept Your Teachings as mine.

19. O God! Paltry and scorned am I
    But my faith in You is strong.
Infinite is Your Righteousness; my devotion to Your Law is lifelong.

20. O God! At dawn I awoke in tears
    Heartfelt was my emotion
I pleaded, Save Your loyal servant. Your Torah is my devotion.

21. O God! Rescue me from my affliction,
    A victim am I of persecution.
Your Torah is Sterling and True, Pure Breath 'midst moral pollution.

22. O God! How faithful have I been to Your Torah
    Daily do I Your praises voice.
I pray that you Save me. In Your every Word I rejoice.

23. O God! Let my weeping reach Your Ears;
    Wipe away my tears.
My heart and hands reach out to help others. To Your Law
                             my soul adheres.

            Despite my cares living by the Torah's words
                       brings me close to God.

Psalm 120. The poet, a pilgrim, prays for deliverance.

        Shalom pilgrims. Jerusalem beckons.

There are those who taint our souls;
    Their lips lie; their tongues defame.
We are surrounded by menacing neighbors.
    Trembling we walk the path to Zion to honor You.
We plead with You, O God, to Punish them.
    War is their goal; peace is our aim. Favor us.

            Troubled pilgrims present their case to God.

Psalm 121. The poet, a pilgrim, prays for God's Protection.

        Shalom pilgrims. Jerusalem beckons.

How we sigh; distressed and in pain are we.
    Where O where will help come from? Mystic Mountain Stirs
                                the wind
    That Rustles the leaves of the trees:
God Ever Awake Will never Forsake Israel! Israel is safe.

            God is Guardian of Israel now
                    and forevermore.

Psalm 122. The poet invites the pilgrims to praise God who Granted them Jerusalem.

        Shalom pilgrims. Jerusalem beckons.

Happy feet have we standing at Zion's gate;
    Joyous souls have we reuniting with kin from other tribes.
We all sing out, Zion is restored;
    We all chant, Jerusalem is safe.

Part Five

Witnesses are we to God's Greatness
    And join to sing thanks
        In the Holy Temple
            In this Sacred Space
                Within these ancient walls.
Under a canopy of peace
    Kith and kin join
        Friends and foe merge
            Victors and vanquished coalesce.
Raise your voices all peoples
    And rejoice in God's Gift.

            Standing at the edge of Jerusalem all peoples
                testify to God's Greatness.

Psalm 123. The poet asks the pilgrims to join in a prayer of Mercy.

    Shalom pilgrims. Jerusalem beckons.

As a servant looks up to master in awe
    Our eyes open to behold Your Majesty O God.
We entreat You be Gracious unto us
    For we are surrounded by scornful tyrants.
Thwart their designs; Foil their plans.
    Spare us; Save us from the clutches of the haughty.

            Pilgrims seek God's Mercy and Protection.

Psalm 124. The poet thanks God for Delivering the people of Israel.

    Shalom pilgrims. Jerusalem beckons.

O God! Without You on our side
    We would still be slaves,
        The raging floods would have drowned us,
            Our enemies would have swallowed us alive.
But You Saved us.
    You Freed us from the snares of foes and the violence of Nature.
        We thank You for Delivering us from danger.

            We thank God that we are not slaves,
            victims of ferocious foes, and of
                  overwhelming forces.

Psalm 125. The poet again thanks God for Delivering the people of Israel.

        Shalom pilgrims. Jerusalem beckons.

As the mountains surround Jerusalem
    So God Surrounds the people of Israel.
They who trust in God are steadfast
    And abide forever in Holiness.
Who but God Makes the crooked straight?
    Who but God Makes the haughty humble?
        Who but God Makes the warlike peace-loving?
The upright shall dwell in the House of God forever.

        Enduring loyalty to God is firm and God's
        Protection is never-failing.

Psalm 126. The poet is excited about the return to Zion.

        Shalom pilgrims. Jerusalem beckons.

When God Restored the Lion of Judah to Zion
    It was a dream come true; it was a time long overdue.
How our melancholy mouths with laughter filled; how our yearning
        hearts for You were fulfilled.
    We began our lives again; we sought to make them better than
        they were when
    We were exiled. We smiled,
        We wept. In peace we slept.
In sorrow we sowed our seeds of a renewed nation
    And we harvested with great elation.
We sang; we prayed; we were no longer afraid.
    At long last we were Home; never again to be forced to roam.

        Overjoyed the exiles were to return
        to Jerusalem.

Psalm 127. The poet praises God for Help Given.

        Shalom pilgrims. Jerusalem beckons.

It is time to rebuild the Holy City!
    In vain are your labors without the Help of God

Watching over you day and night.
>The greatest blessings in God's Sight are the children
With minds sparkling with wisdom and with eloquent tongues.
>God Plants the Roots of Goodness in Parents
Who then sow the seeds of maturity in their Children
>Who, thriving, then bestow them on their children
>>for all generations.

>>*Blesséd are the children, Gifts of God,*
>>>*who renew all that is holy.*

Psalm 128. The poet declares that happiness IS FOLLOWING GOD'S WAYS.

>Shalom pilgrims. Jerusalem beckons.

Blesséd are they who revere God;
>They walk in the way of the upright.
Work with your hands; earn your bread
>And all in your household will be happy and well fed.
God Blesses you from Zion
>And Opens your eyes to see the glory of Jerusalem.
You who return to Zion.
>Be strong like lion, wise like sages, virtuous like the righteous,
>>and merciful like God.
>May you live to see your grandchildren prosper.

>>*Sow the seeds of peace and receive*
>>>*God's Blessing.*

Psalm 129. The poet asks Israel's foes to change their ways.

>Shalom pilgrims. Jerusalem beckons.

How sorely have I been afflicted from the days of my youth;
>But I was not defeated.
Like farmers tilling a field my soul has been sundered and furrowed
>But I was not deleted.
My trust is in God.
>You who despise Zion give up your evil designs and instead
>>glorify one another.
Those who honor each other are Blessed by God.

Essence of the Psalms

> *Israel hopes that through trust in God*
> *all peoples will live in peace.*

Psalm 130. The poet atones and seeks God's Redemption.

> Shalom pilgrims. Jerusalem beckons.

O God! Out of the depths of my soul I call upon You. I have strayed.
> Help me.
    My soul weeps; my heart aches.
Hear the pith of my very being rejoice
    Knowing that You Hearken unto my imploring voice.
What mortal is completely without fault? Who has not drifted
> from Your Path?
    But You are the Root of Mercy and the Peak of Pardon.
We learn from Your Guidance; we redirect our steps to receive
> Your Love.
    O God, My Redeemer, we await Your Forgiveness.

> *Israel having drifted from the God's Precepts*
> *corrects its ways and awaits*
> *God's Grace.*

Psalm 131. The poet sings a song of solace.

> Shalom pilgrims. Jerusalem beckons.

O Merciful God! Smugness and vanity ebb from my heart.
    A placid calm flows within me
I am content: what I own is enough.
    Like a child in its mother's bosom I rejoice in my lot.

> *How happy are they who are satisfied with*
> *themselves. They know peace.*

Psalm 132. The poet says that David prepared a Place for God to Dwell in Zion.

> Shalom pilgrims. Jerusalem beckons.

O All Knowing God !
    You Fathom how sorely distressed

Part Five

Was Your servant David
    With whom You Made a pact
To find a place, a Holy Place,
    Where You Will Abide.
Food lost its flavor; life lost its savor.
    Sleep was strained; his soul was pained.
Then in the very heart of Jerusalem
    In the very marrow of its soul
David found a Sacred Space, a Holy Place
    Where You Will Abide Where You will Preside.
A Place where all who are devout, clothed in goodness,
    Will sing and dance.
There will You Care for the needy and Clothe the naked.
    And You Will Anoint the king,
His crown Radiant with Your Blessing,
    To rule over Israel.
And enemies, clothed in shame,
    Will repent and worship Adonai, God's Holy Name.

        Jerusalem becomes a dwelling for God.

Psalm 133. The poet praises the unity of people.

    Shalom pilgrims. Jerusalem beckons.

How good and pleasant it is to dwell together in peace and harmony.

        There is no gift of Nature that can compare
            with the symmetry of human
            solidarity.

Psalm 134. The poet praises God day and night.

    Shalom pilgrims. Jerusalem beckons.

May all who worship God
    Be blessed in holy places
Raise your arms to pray
    Every day and every night
In pitch-black darkness, in brightest light.
    God Who Stretched out the heavens and Made Fertile the earth
        Bless us all from Zion.

        How grateful are we to the Author

of the universe.

Psalm 135. The poet praises God for Goodness and Strength

Halleluyah. Praise Adonai, our God.
    Praise God's Holy Name;
        Daily proclaim the Wonders God Wrought.
All who worship God
    Laud, extol, exalt, glorify, and magnify.
All who serve God
    Your lives are not bitter but sweet
        Your lives are not empty but complete.
God Chose Jacob as a treasure who, after a struggle, became Israel.
    His children were pioneers, gems beyond measure,
Whose offspring were spared in Egypt
    Then given Canaan as a Heritage.
O God, Just and Kind,
    You are not like pagan gods
Made by smiths, masons, and potters.
    You Make lightning, wind, and rain
You Guide farmers in season to sow
    Fruits and vegetables that grow
And feed peoples everywhere.
    We know You Care.
Daily we pause to praise You
    Who Abides in Jerusalem.
Your Name is a living memorial
    Every generation in every nation will revere it.

        There is One Living God Who Looks after
        Jacob's issue.

Psalm 136. The poet praises God's Gifts.

We thank You God, Author of the Universe
    Who Made the heavens;
        Who Spread the earth above the waters;
Who Commanded the sun to rule by day and the moon and stars
        to brighten the night;
    Who Saved Israel from the cruel hand of Pharaoh;
        Who Led the Children of Israel out of Egypt across the

Part Five

                                        waters into the wilderness;
    Who Gave them the land of Canaan as a Heritage;
      Who Fed the hungry and Clothed the naked;
              Who Lifted our spirits in our darkest moments;
   Who Sustained and Maintained all who follow the Torah, a Beacon
                                  of Light;
       Who Tends and Nourishes us and Brings us joy.
          Who daily Shows every Kindness.
                How Good and Magnificent You Are.
             Your Mercy Endures forever.

        Endless are God's Virtues.

Psalm 137. The poet laments the Exile.

As we sat by the waters of Babylon
    Our thoughts turned to Zion
And we wept bitter tears
    For days, for months, for years.

Our tormentors taunted us
    Why don't you sing your beloved songs of Zion?
But Exile purges
    And all we could sing were dirges.

Our lyres hang in limbo
    There are no songs to sing in a foreign land.
O Jerusalem I must never forget you.
    My love for you is true.

There will come a day
    And that day will be soon,
When once again we will be free
    When we'll taste the sweet nectar of liberty.

        How the exiled yearned to return to Zion.

Psalm 138. The poet laments the destruction of the temple.

O God! From the nub of my soul
    And from the hub of my heart
I speak Your Name
    And declaim Your Virtues.
In anguish and in joy

> I call You Adonai, my God.
> And You Answer me.
>> You Give me Courage and Resolve
> To cope with Life's strains
>> And to allay Life's pains.
> Who after all am I? No king, no prince, no rich merchant.
>> I am just a lowly mortal.
> Still I am a special someone to You.
>> When I walk in the midst of trouble
> You Guide me to safety.
>> As long as I live I will serve You.

God is ever with us no matter our station in life.

Psalm 139. The poet praises the Ever-present God.
> O God! I barely know myself
>> Yet You Understand me thoroughly.
> Whether I am far or near
>> Whether in joy or fear
> Whether awake or sleeping
>> Whether smiling or weeping.
> Before a word slips from my tongue, You Know it.
>> Before a thought from my mind is sprung,
> You Know it.
>> You have enclosed me; I cannot run away from You.
> Wherever I turn, You are there;
>> Cloaked in darkness, You Find me. In the pit,
> You Find me.
>> Across the sea, You Find me.
> On a mountain top, You Find me. In the driest desert, You Find me.
>> You are my Guide, My Shelter, my Teacher, my Compass.
> If I err, stay Your Wrath; if I stray, Redirect my path.
>> All Knowing God, Teach me Your Wisdom.

Disciples of God are we.

Part Five

Psalm 140. The poet prays for Deliverance from enemies.

O God! Rescue me from evil people; Spare me from their violence.
    Daily they start many a war;
        Their tongues the innocent gore;
            Their mouths with venom fill;
                Their hands innocent blood spill.
                    They build traps and snares;
                        I trip, my heart despairs.
Still I cry out to You my God,
    Hear my words. I am awed
By Your Power of Love;
    I know You Watch from Your Abode All Around and Above.
Cleanse the world of those who would evil pursue;
    Evil passions in all I plead You Subdue.
Don't Let evildoers succeed
    Their harmful designs Impede.
Send Your Mercy and Wisdom from on High
    Teach us how Your World to sanctify.

*   God's Mercy and Wisdom can turn evildoers*
*   into doers of good.*

Psalm 141. The poet prays to be spared from doing wrong.

O God! Do You Hear me?
    Answer quickly. It is urgent.
Let me not be lured into telling lies.
    Let me not be tempted into ways I despise.
When I lapse Rebuke me;
    When I speak guile Reproach my folly.
So that I not utter evil, seal my lips with a guard;
    So that I not do evil acts, let all weapons be barred.
There are hateful leaders, punish them;
    There are scheming kings, condemn them.
Let all who befoul their coronets
    Become ensnared in their own nets.
All I seek is Heavenly Renewal;
    You are my Crown, I am Your jewel.

*   God's Wisdom Guides us away from evil*
*   and toward virtue.*

Psalm 142. The poet petitions God to Deliver David from evildoers.

    A skillful song of David.

My voice pours out my agony with every breath
    My mouth implores You, "Protect me."
I plead. Heed my cry.
    My spirit languishes.
I lay before You my complaint;
    I am beset by foes who set traps for me.
I am alone. No mortal cares about me.
    I despair.
You surely Know this. O God, My Refuge!
    Free my soul from its prison.
O that the upright will encircle me;
    O that we are enveloped in the Crown of Your Bounty.

    Alone and hopeless only God Will Listen.

Psalm 143. The poet prays for deliverance.

    A Song in David's name.

My enemies pursue me and drain me of spirit;
    My foes hunt me down and crush my will.
O God! Hear my torment and suffering;
    Ponder my misery and agony.
Needles prick my soul; arrows lance my body.
    Speak to me God in my prison;
Liberate me from my jail.
    Give me water in this arid place that parches my mouth;
I languish, I weaken, I fade without Your Protection.
    I remember when I was young
I marveled at Your Creation
    And meditated upon Your Kindness.
Show me Your Mercy again.
    I will follow the Path You Map out for me;
I will keep Your Laws.
    O God ! You are Just;
In You I give my total trust.
    O Merciful One Do not Permit my foes to harass me.

Part Five

O Kindly One Destroy the evil impulse
    And Let all be deemed innocent before You.

*Suffering is a part of life but following
God's Path restores one.*

Psalm 144. The poet petitions God to Save the people.
    A Psalm in honor of David

O God! Rock and Source of Strength! We are surrounded by
        ferocious foes
    Who from their mean spirits venom flows.
        Teach our minds to ignore each offense; Teach our tongues
            harmony to dispense;
        Teach our fists self-defense.

Our lives are so fragile; in a matter of seconds our breath is like
        vapor gone.
    What is a person after all?
        A trivial droplet of water in the ocean?
            A paltry grain of sand on the beach?
                A mere mote of dust in the cosmos?
                    A comma in Your Annals?
                      A speck in Eternity?
No each of us is an individual, a Sacred Being, Blessed by You,
    Ordained to do justice and mercy
        And to teach them to others.
O God of Nature Who Scatters the Lightning like arrows
    And who Makes mountains explode from a fiery earth
Raise us from the abyss into which we have fallen
    And free us from the foes who blacken our names.
Despite our suffering we pluck the strings of our lyres
    And sing a new song unto You.
Rescue us! Raise us out of the pit.
    We pray with all our hearts
That our children grow up to be vibrant pillars of the community
    And like date palms sweeten the land of milk
    and honey.
How rich will we be; our storehouses will be in full supply.
    And happy are they whose God is Adonai.

*Those who pray to God will be free, saved,
and happy.*

Psalm 145. The poet declares the Greatness of God.

O God! Every evening and every morning I marvel at the Wonders
of Creation.
What Splendor! What Grandeur! What Peerless Beauty.
I praise Your Glorious Name.
I kindle the Torch of Compassion
That You Have Passed to me and I bestow unto
my children
To tell them that You Listen to their hearts filled with anguish.
Your Mercy is Tender and Your Justice is Fair.
I join the holy ones to praise
Your Endless Power to Do Good.
The hungry are fed; the naked clothed; the ailing, healed;
the fallen lifted up.
O God! Banish Evil and Broadcast seeds of Goodness.

*Let every creature bless Your Majestic Name
forever.*

Psalm 146. The poet thanks God for Caring and for the Wonders of Creation.

My soul echoes with praises to You, O God,
Guardian of Truth,
The Very Essence of Justice ,
Protector of the stranger,
Keeper of the orphan,
Warden of the widow.
You Feed the hungry,
You Clothe the naked,
You Redeem the refugee,
You Support the fallen,
You Sustain the stranger,
You Give Sight to the blind,
And Sound to the deaf.
You Make the crooked straight and from a void Create
A world of wonder:
The heavens, the mountains and the seas;
The birds and the beasts,
And Cures for disease.

Part Five

Princes can be corrupted, they are not to be trusted.
    Even the most honest have no power
        After they are laid in their graves.
            I put my faith in You O Eternal One, Source of
            Virtue and Grace.
Before I enter the world of Silence Where my body will turn to dust
        I sing to You, O Majestic King,
            I pray that You Will Reign in the Cosmos Forever
        and Ever.
               Halleluyah. God Be Praised.

                  Every day you look to God, Source of The
                            Ideal, for Inspiration.

Psalm 147. The poet praises God, Guardian of Jerusalem, Mentor of World Peace.

How good it is to sing praises unto God,
    Who Rebuilds Jerusalem,
        Who Gathers in the dispersed,
            Who Gleans the sorrows of the anguished,
                Who Gives balm to the broken heart,
                      Who Heals the bankrupt soul.
How pleasant it is to sing praises unto God,
    Who Stretches out the Heavens,
        Who Names the stars,
            Who Is Infinite,
                Who Is All-Powerful,
                      Who Rescues the needy.
How joyous it is to give thanks unto God,
    Who Provides rain in season,
        Who Feeds the animals,
            Who Delights in those who pray at the holy shrine,
                Who Blesses those who revere The Divine.
O God! Show us how to make peace at our borders;
    O God! Teach us how to curb anger and find love in our hearts.
        Send forth Words of Comfort to the bereaved;
            Plant Your Wisdom in our minds as farmers
                      sow their crops.

Do princes deserve our trust?
> Fleeting is their time on earth.
>> Are kings known to be just
>>> When they from their promises retreat?
But You, O God, are Majestic;
> You are Just, Merciful, Infallible, and Eternal.
>> Your Laws are Guides to the lost
>>> And Beacons to the storm-tossed.
>>>> Halleluyah. God Be Praised.

God's Mercy Permeates Nature and Society.

Psalm 148. The poet calls on all to praise God.

In the beginning there was Silence.
> Then from a distance the crisp tones of sopranos lofted high
>> And after a moment in Time
>>> Were joined in harmony by the dulcet strains
>>>> of the altos.
>>> After another moment in Time
>>>> The melodic tenors added their voices
>>>>> And, finally, the deep basses set
>>>>>> the rhythm.

Young and old; men and women; princes and kings,
> Beggar, widow, and orphan,
>> Student, teacher, and merchant
>>> All sang praises to God.

And in their own ways the creatures roaming the land praised God
> As did those who soar in the air,
> As did those who swim in the sea.

Then from a distance in Time and Space
> The sun, the moon, and the stars chanted their praise.
>> The angels joined by the Heavenly Legions caroled
>>> Halleluyah. Halleluyah. Halleluyah.
>>>> God Be Praised.

And Divine Rays Beamed throughout the Cosmos to Honor
>>>> all who are Holy
> For they are Belovéd of God.
>> And together they chanted
>>> Halleluyah.

All Creation, Reflections of the Divine,
> *Give Praises to God.*

Part Five

Psalm 149. The poet celebrates Israel's victory over its enemies.

Sing a new song unto God
    Chant a benediction; voice it with conviction.
        Sing it in the fields; sing it in the homes; sing it
            at the holy shrine,
Let The Children of Israel join all Children of God, to show their
            delight in the Divine
    By dancing with harp and by marching with timbrel.
God Adorns the humble with redemption;
    God Bedecks the lowly with liberation.
All God's Children extol this day
    Because their foes are in disarray.
            A day has arrived when Israel
            revels in victory.

Psalm 150. The poet extols God's Greatness.

How Mighty are God's Deeds; how praiseworthy.
    Blow the shofar; clash the cymbals; beat the drum, pluck the harp.
           (shofar-ram's horn)
    Sing! Dance!
Let everything and everyone with breath
    Praise God.
    Halleluyah. Halleluyah. Halleluyah. Praise be to God.

        The day has arrived when all peoples praise
        God's Mighty Power.
    Be of good courage! Strengthen yourself to perform
        the Word of God.

Section Two

Modern Psalms

1. **The poet declares that The Essence of God is within us.**

   God Eternal, Friend and Guide,
       Dwell within us sanctified:
   Calm as oceans, deep and blue
       And strong as mountains, tall and true.
   Enfold us with Divine Embrace;
       Invest in us Your Loving Grace;
   And Grant us mind that we will know
       The Paths of Right for us to go.
   Almighty God each day we extol
       Your Gifts of body, mind, and soul.
   With likeness to Your Very Own
       Whose Seeds we sow as You Have Sown.

       Mortals strive to be virtuous like God.

2. **The poet praises God's Works and asks that mortals improve their ways.**

   It is You God Painting patterns on summer flowers
       And Tinting birds in exquisite display.
   And Building the tallest mountains
       And Renewing the sun every day.

   It is You God Filling the oceans
       And Drawing the rivers to the seas.
   And Makings plants to nourish the body
       And Giving taste to fruit of trees.

   But God You Witness wrongdoing everywhere
       In every land You Behold its curse.
   I pray You Teach human hearts to act justly
       And our straying ways to Reverse.

       Awesome Are God's Works but Mortals tarnish them.

       Improve God's World by doing good works.

3. The poet praises God, The Guiding Light.

Almighty God, Blessed be Your Name. Beacon of Wisdom.
>   Counsel and Guide us to become
Friendly amid alienation, dignified amid arrogance,
>   Merciful amid cruelty, truthful amid deceit,
Builders amid destruction, able amid helplessness,
>   Forgiving amid insult, modest amid pretension,
Generous amid selfishness, striving amid struggle,
>   Considerate amid carelessness, calm amid turmoil,
Fair amid injustice, believing amid falseness,
>   Hopeful amid despair, and loving amid hatred.

Despite our trials we ask God to Raise us to a higher standard.

4. The poet prays to God to Renew in us the Gift of Life.

In this world as Your guest I dwell.
>   'Tis not for long; just for a spell.
When my life fulfills its time
>   I'll thank You God for Your Gift Sublime.

Although life is finite it is noble.

5. The poet, distressed, finds God nearby and is rescued.

I beseeched you God in my duress
>   To Raise me from the depths of distress.
Menaced was I by sinister forces.
>   How could I cope? I lacked resources.
Anger flooded my anguished soul
>   I prayed Stanch its flow and Make me whole.
Then You, The Blesséd and Sanctified,
>   Was there by my side
Teaching my mind Your Way to Live:
>   To revere each Gift that You Give.
Thank you God for what You Have Done
>   You've Taken my parts and made me one.

God Rescues us from our suffering.

6. The poet recounts Where God is Found.

I find You God in cryptic genes,
> In leafy greens, in disease vaccines.

I find You God in morning skies,
> In fireflies, in newborns' cries.

I find You God in oceans deep,
> In woolly sheep, in cats that leap.

I find You God in mountains tall,
> In babes who crawl, in rains that fall.

I find Your Art in each of these,
> And when I do my mind's at ease.

But when I view Man's heart in course ,
> Your Kind Compassion, Once its Source,

Has been expelled by human pride.
> I beseech You God to Return us to Your Side.

God is everywhere to be found. We only have to search.

7. The poet understands God's Agony.

God how full of Agony You must Be
> To See the evil Your creatures do to each other.

God how full of Remorse You must Be
> To Witness Your children killing one another.

The errors of mortals distress God.

8. The poet asks God to Bless all mortals.

God Eternal, Source of Grace,
> Bless each child of every race

With Kindly Love towards each other
> To share each day with one another.

God Cherishes the chaste child.

9. The poet asks prays earnestly to God.

O God of all Creation
> Hearken to my meditation.
> All about me are the iniquitous
> Whose evil ways are ubiquitous.

Cheering Your Name
They kill and maim.
> They kneel and pray
> Then shout and slay.

Do you Abhor such conceit?
Do you Condemn such deceit?
> Their worship is flawed and also tainted,
> Not the prayers of the sainted.

Shield not those who Your Words pervert;
Save them not who Your Laws subvert.
> Stand by the humble and the just;
> Protect those who in You do trust.

Let the poor in spirit no longer fret;
Let the righteous live no longer under threat.
> Mend the souls of those who are caring;
> Heal the spirits of those despairing.

Daub with balm each pleading face;
Send to each your radiant Grace.
> The evil deeds of the wicked undo.
> And Bless the poor, the hurt, the true.

Pray that God Annuls evil and Comfort the ill-treated.

10. The poet, once forlorn, knows through God there is Renewal.

My life was a desolate island
> Ravaged by a raging storm

My soul was a hollow cavern
> Worn away by hate.

My heart bled with heated anger;
> My mouth hemorrhaged hateful words.

My mind sunk in despair;
> My brain doomed every promise.

Then Rain like Tears from heaven
> Washed my filthy past.

Next I saw golden daffodils
> And an eagle soaring high;

I watched a mother feeding her young
> And a cobalt sky passing by. I knew that tomorrow

Would be better than today
> Because You God are Hope Eternal
And Renew us everyday.
> *God Imbues the soul with hope.*

11. The poet focuses on God, the Lodestar of prayer.

The center of my ardent prayer
> Is filled with sunshine and purest air.
Glowing fish swim the streams that flow;
> Golden palms sway as zephyrs blow.
Speckled birds in trees build nests
> Guarding young from hostile pests.
Roses embroider the edges with hue,
> Spreading scents they so well brew.
Hand in hand with God I walk
> In this garden we silently talk.
When our tidings are at an end,
> I say "Amen" to my Constant Friend.
As the Gates of Prayer start to close,
> The Presence of God about me Glows.

> *God Listens to our prayers and Guides our actions.*

12. The poet asks God for Solace.

God I beseech You to Grant me
> Solace to get through this day.
>> And when night swallows the sun's last ray
>>> Grant peace of soul and set me free.

> *Serenity is God's Gift day and night.*

13. The poet opens the door to God's Treasury.

I hid in my room under siege of fear
> Watching my bright flame disappear.
My soul, full-grown, began to shrink;
> My brain, once nimble, could not think.
I could not eat, I'd only weep
> In bed at night I could not sleep.

Friends and kin would talk to me,
    But all I heard was calumny.
Then a Voice Whispered Lovingly,
    "Halt your self-indulgent misery.
Walk outside and see My Light;
    My flowers in bloom; My birds in flight."
I shuffled my feet in apathy
    Then opened the door to a Treasury
Of Sights, and Sounds, and Touch, and Smells
    And realized that the Living God within me Dwells.
A God that Listens, a God that Cares
    A God that Trusts and Ne'er Despairs.
Teach me God soul salvation:
    Mercy, Kindness, and Consecration.
Today I listen, today I care
    Today I trust without despair.
God's my Friend ever True
    And Kindles my flame each day anew.

        God Lifts souls out of the depths of despair
        to the height of hope.

14. The poet implores us to enjoy God's Heritage.

With cuppéd hands upon our eyes,
    Witnesses all, as one we rise.
Joining forbears whom we mourn
    And descendants not yet born
To sing this anthem every day:
    The call to worship we obey.
You are our God, the only One
    All that's Sacred from You has Come.
In hushéd tones we bless Your Name
    And Your Glorious Kingdom we proclaim.
We chant the words of the Holy Writ,
    A Heritage that we to our children transmit:
From You Springs our might.
    We will love You every day and every night.
We'll show kindness every place we go,
    Where hills rise high; where streams gently flow.

Yours is the Law which Sows the Seeds
    That Blossom into righteous deeds.
I'll Inscribe It on the gates of mind:
    Eternal temple where You are enshrined.

The Sacred Words of God are always within us.

15. The poet changes outlook and deeds.

I sat forlorn in my darkened room
    Filled with rancor, wallowing in gloom.
I'd thought of ills that were done to me
    And expected to receive more calumny.
Within me rose shouting voices,
    "Stop self pity, you have two choices,
Either sit there and forge barbed curses
    Or recite for others some cheerful verses."
I admit I had the thirst
    To form some barbs and do the first.
"That's morose" my hot brain reckoned
    So I opened my lips and did the second.
I changed my aim, and reset my goal.
    I prayed to God to free my soul.
My soul from my own jail was then set free,
    And I became who I want to be.
I no longer acted the thorny cactus.
    All day long good deeds I'd practice.
When I donned a happy face
    I could feel, Dear God, Your Warm Embrace.

A cheerful outlook brings one close to God.

16. The poet views yesterdays as gone and tomorrows to be uncertain.

Strolling the beach at the height of noon
    Perched atop the tallest dune,
I look behind at yesterday,
    The footprints made have blown away.
When I turn to regard tomorrow,
    The path's unclear for me to follow.

What is mine and yours for sure is just this day
    In which to seek a better way.
So be guided by the sun
    And share its warmth with everyone
Because soon the winds and the moon-drawn tide
    Will swallow the dune we've occupied.

This day is ours to share with all.

17. The poet says that the deeds of the righteous are exquisite.

Is the taste of ripe pears not succulent? Is the scent of lilacs not fragrant?
    So are the deeds of the righteous. So are the good works
        of the virtuous.

Savor the deed and actions of the righteous.

18. The poet asks God to Give lessons in coping with the future.

In anguish I sleep every night; with woe I awake each morn.
    How I fear what is to come;
Yet what mortal can ever Death's meaning plumb?
    O God! Font of Compassion, Source of Mercy,
Teach me to endure what is destined to be.
    Send me Comfort in my despair and Teach my arid soul to thrive.

The uncertainty and travail in life can be
*   overcome with acceptance.*

19. The poet sings sweetly to God.

With song do I sing Your praises,
    With sweetness like the nightingale.
        With joy my voice to You raises,
            Dissolving my tearful travail.

Mending are the melodies sung to God.

20. The poet announces that the upright improve the world.

Search and look throughout the land
    In waters deep, in desert sand
For diamonds treasured above the rest
    And for rubies valued as the best.

Modern Psalms

Look for these among those who pray
> In what they do, in what they say.
Found are they in souls of the pure
> Whose goodness will world's sorrows cure.
Temper the raging, hurtful crowd
> And set free in us Your Love Endowed.

> > *Troves of cures for world's cares are in*
> > *the veins in the upright.*

21. The poet's misdeeds are thrown to the waters.

Into the river I throw my failings,
> They disappear with the floating debris.
As I pour out to You my sincere confessions, I know that You
> > Listen to me;
> Because freed am I of my oppressions, released am I
> > of self-tyranny.

> > *Casting flaws to the waters cleanses the soul.*

22. The poet asks God to Help us correct our wrongs.

Locusts have devoured our crops
> Deer have chewed our trees
The drought has dried our wheat
> The hot winds have killed our bees.
We have no more grains to eat,
> No more honey sweeten our tongues
Sound the alarm, pray, and fast
> Polluted air fills our lungs.
Injustice defiles us;
> Eating away at our very core;
Help us reform our wayward habits
> And to Your Grace to soar.

> > *Following God's Path undoes the damage*
> > *we do in this world.*

23. The poet is awed by the Wonders God Created.

At first the earth was unformed and void
    And Your Spirit Hovered over the face of the waters.
And then there was Light.
    Then, the waters were divided
So that there were waters below the firmament
    And waters above the firmament.
Next there was dry land as well as waters
    And the dry land put forth herbs and grasses,
And fruit as well as nut bearing trees.
    Then came the light that reigned by day
Followed by lights seen only by night.
    Then there were creatures swarming about the land:
Wingéd creatures, all kinds of fish that swarmed in the deep
    And horses, cattle, sheep, felines, canines, and simians.
Then when all of this was completed
    You Contemplated and Meditated, You had Reservations
                      but Resolve
And You Created the human family
    Endowed with temptation and the will to subdue it,
Endowed with Emotion and the will to control it through thought,
    Endowed with language and the will to use it to record history,
Endowed with Charity and the will to help others.
    And then You Rested. It was the Sabbath, the Crown
                      of Your Creation.
Who but You God could Create a wonder-filled world
    So almost perfect that humans, made in Your Image,
Deriving Compassion, Wisdom, and Righteousness from You
    Are given the duty to complete and preserve Creation.

How filled with marvel is God's World.

24. The poet asks God, Giver of Goodness, to Reveal the roots of evil.

God, my love for You is enduring; God, unblemished is my trust.
    Long have I pondered about the evil in the world;
Long have I wondered about wrongdoing and deceit.
    It is said that we in Your Image have been created,
It is said that Your Character we have imitated.
    But no, it cannot be!

With determined heart I disagree!
    What You have Given to us as Bequest,
Most important above all the rest,
    Are the acts of kindness that we do
And the goodwill to others that we foster, too.
    But You have Given to us a choice
And I have listened to Your Sapient Voice.
    After thinking my quandary through and through
I have discovered the answer which I hold true:
    The wicked have Your Virtues rejected,
But the righteous have Your Virtues accepted.

        The upright trust in and cultivate God's Way.

25. The poet's Prayer Echoes in Heaven.

The melody that from one's soul does spring
    In heaven above resounds
And to God, The Divine, humbly does bring
    A blessing which to Earth rebounds.

        God Accepts and Returns our worship.

26. The poet forges a partnership with God.

God of the patriarchs and of the matriarchs,
    Great, Glorious, and Awesome,
        We join You as partners in renewing creation to
            Feed the hungry
                Clothe the naked
                    House the homeless,
                Heal the sick,
                        Mend the broken in spirit;
                            Wash the unbathed,
                      Strengthen the weak,
                Ease the oppressed,
            Give hope to the despairing,
            And comfort the mourner.

Help us Teach the wrongdoer Your Ways of righteousness;
    Help us Teach the greedy to be content with their lot;
        Help us Teach the ignorant to cherish learning;
            Help us Teach the solemn how to smile;

Help us Teach the merrymaker how to cry;
    Help us Set goals with the aimless;
    Help us Give work to the unemployed;
    And Help us Open the eyes of all to see the Beauty
        of Creation.
Each of us is Your Child; No matter how old we are or
    how we dress;
Each of us is Your child; no matter what color is our skin;
Each of us is Your child; no matter where and how we pray;
Each of us is Your child; No matter what others say.

*There are many ways we can work with God
to improve the world.*

27. The poet urges that listening to God can transform us.

O God! In silent pauses we hear Your Voice
    Soaring to Grant peace and serenity
        To every heart raging from everyday life;
Rising to fill with The Sublime our ears muddled
    With the cacophony of the commonplace.
Oh God, Open our eyes to see Your Glory
    That Changes drab banality into strands of silver and gold;
Oh God, Open our ears to hear Your Truths
    Guide us to a Higher Level of Virtue.
Oh God, Open our hearts to receive Your Love
    That Heals the anguished world.

*Through God is there Peace, Beauty, Truth
and Caring.*

28. The poet is transformed.

Surrounded by the bleak, blackness of night I writhed in wretchedness;
    frantic with fretting.
Then I heard my breath, sensed my pulsing heart, and awoke
    lusting for life.
My eyes opened to the chaste, unadorned, simplicity and goodness
    of Light;
To the ancient, still shining , and constantly renewing sun;

To the iridescence and flapping of the wings of birds
    Whose forebears soared mutating and adapting to a
                    changing planet;
To the sweet, savor of attar of roses whose satin petals stir the senses
    With their bouquet of eternal purity.
At that moment, at that very moment, 'neath a glittering astral canopy,
    Unmasked, I entered the present stripped of all distractions,
                  bare of all camouflages,
Empty of all pretense.
    And I watched the TO BE become the NOW and, in a tick
                of Time, the THEN.
And I gazed at tiny flickers of threads of candlelight
    Consisting of countless, colorful, undulating, gyrating surges
                of vitality,
With its tiniest caloric output, heat space and expand it.
    Then I became part of the cosmos and the cosmos became
                part of me.

Immersion in Creation is a conversion experience.

29. The poet imbibes the Sabbath Spirit.

Drink in the glory of Sabbath, elixir of hope
    When tenderness shines as an eternal light
        At the Bosom of the living God.
    Let peace feed every cell of our beings
And fill us with warmth, with healing, with wisdom, with caring,
                and with joy.

The Sabbath is a conversion experience.

30. The poet declares that the Sabbath sparkles with God's Light.

The mounting flickers of Sabbath candles
    Sends light back to God to brighten the universe.
        Sabbath day transforms Time.
                The light of the candles illuminate our souls
        And florets of peace open into a rainbow of color
    More lustrous than diamonds;
More sparkling than sapphires.

Sabbath Time Glistens with Holiness.

31. The poet finds peace on the Sabbath.

'Round and 'round the Earth has spun
   In endless trek about the sun.
      Now as evening shadows fall
         Wrapping Earth in dusky shawl,
            The remaining plumes of feathered light
               Dissolve inside the approaching night.
                  Welcome Sabbath which God has Blessed
              And Ordained for all a day of rest.
          Six days we've toiled and we've languished;
     At life we've roiled and we've anguished.
   As the silvered moon rises all cares cease.
  Then our souls find Sabbath Peace
And from every care we find release.

              The Sabbath Cleanses our beings of
                       daily plights.

32. The poet prays for God's Healing.

Oh Divine Healer Who Listens
   To the distress and despair of all
      Soothe and Comfort our ailing bodies
         Oust the barbs and stings of our pain
            Remove the shackles from our minds;
               Banish the fetters that bind our souls.
            Grant affliction wings to fly away;
         Drop it into the sea.
      Command the rising swells to swallow
   And dissolve it until it vanishes.
With Your Divine Healing, Brighten the day of all who suffer.

Then let the seeds of our joy blossom and prosper.
     Raise us to a higher plane;
        Lift us to a loftier level.
           Mend our broken parts.
         Ordain that we become whole again.
    Restore us; Heal us.
And Your Canopy of Devotion will Hover over us. AMEN.

                    God Allays and Restores us.

33. The poet prays to God to Free us from human frailty.

We pray to You each day, each night,
    We pray to You with all our might
To Sustain our hungry, needy kin
    And Turn our ways away from sin;

To Clothe our naked without a stitch,
    To Teach Compassion to the rich,
To Heal the sick in flesh and mind,
    And to Teach all peoples to be just and kind;

To Protect the vagrants who nightly roam,
    To Shelter those without a home,
To Comfort those in abyss of grief,
    And to those in pain to Give Relief;

To Temper the raging, hurtful crowd,
    To Free in all Your Love Endowed,
To Rid the world of fear and war,
    And to Grant us peace for ever more.

Through God's Love the human condition is improved.

34. The poet asks God for protection.

God, our Refuge and our Hope,
    Protect us, Save us, Redeem us.
Lift melancholy from the mourners;
    Sow tranquility within the anguished;
        Mend the ill in body;
            Teach humility to the arrogant;
                Reveal the concealed good in all.
We sing a new song unto You O God.
    Thanking You for the Gifts You Bestow on us
        For us to share with others.

Ailing humanity can mend with God's Help.

35. The poet says that God Listens to our prayers.

   God Hears our prayers with Tear-Soaked Face
      God Hears our prayers and Grants us Grace.
         But to wipe God's Tears away
            We must save Creation from decay.

            God is Saddened by human vice
            But mortals can make this world a paradise.

36. The poet calls for freedom from self-incrimination.

  Within my brain there is a cell
     Where evil thoughts are jailed,
        An everlasting fiery hell
           Smold'ring with times when I have failed.
  I call upon my refuse truck
     To haul my foul debris
        But it gets stuck in memory muck
           And spills its villainy.
  It flows through ev'ry artery
     Spreading poison along the way
        Until it finds a liturgy
           With sacred words to pray.
  They teach me I have ten billion more
     Cells in which to find
        My noble thoughts to store
           And sanctify my mind.

            Replace reflections of personal failure with
                      sublime meditations.

37. The poet condemns greed and pleads that mortals return to God.

  In these days of moral famine
     There is a common creed
        To genuflect to the priests of Mammon
           And daily practice rites of greed.
  Helping those in desp'rate need
     They call a mortal sin,
        And wounding others until they bleed
           Brings praise and not chagrin.

The time has come to condemn that breed
   That favors gold's glitter to woman and man
      And from Mammon's grip be freed
         And find a place in God's Grand Plan.
            Doing good is its own reward
               It improves one's self and the world.
                  It brings about universal accord
                     And peace far and near is
                        unfurled.

*Replace the pursuit of fortune without regard
to others with noble acts.*

38. The poet sings a song of Thanksgiving.

Thank You God for the morning sun and for the moon when
   day is done,
Thank You for the stars night skies bring, thank You God
   for everything.
Thank You God for the wind and rains that cleanse
   the earth on hills and plains.
Thank You for the blossoms of Spring, thank You God
   for everything.
Thank You God for Laws You Provide and for Your Teaching
   that is our Guide,
Thank You God for the songs angels sing, thank You
   God for everything.
Thank You God for Your Hand in Love and for the Gifts
   from Heav'n above.
Thank You for the peace that You Bring, thank You
   God for Everything.

*How grateful are we for the Largess God
has Bestowed on us.*

Appendix

Appendix

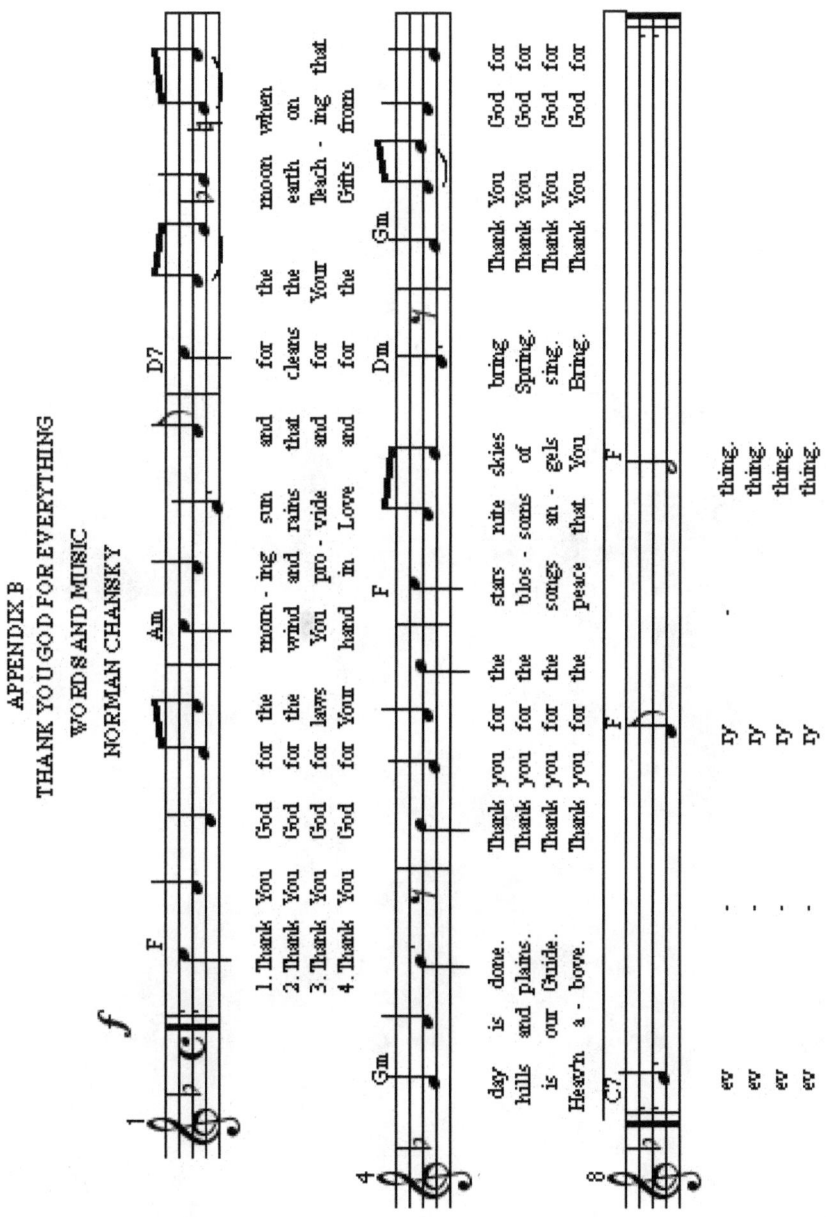

www.ingramcontent.com/pod-product-compliance
Lightning Source LLC
Chambersburg PA
CBHW070925160426
43193CB00011B/1577